THE ELEPHANT GOSPEL

UNSHACKLED TO LIVE THE SECRET OF HOPE

DEBORAH ANN SAINT

WESTBOW
PRESS®
A DIVISION OF THOMAS NELSON
& ZONDERVAN

WestBow Press books may be ordered through booksellers or by contacting:

WestBow Press
A Division of Thomas Nelson & Zondervan
1663 Liberty Drive
Bloomington, IN 47403
www.westbowpress.com
1 (866) 928-1240

Because of the dynamic nature of the Internet, any web addresses or links contained in this book may have changed since publication and may no longer be valid. The views expressed in this work are solely those of the author and do not necessarily reflect the views of the publisher, and the publisher hereby disclaims any responsibility for them.

Any people depicted in stock imagery provided by Thinkstock are models, and such images are being used for illustrative purposes only. Certain stock imagery © Thinkstock.

ISBN: 978-1-5127-6955-5 (sc)
ISBN: 978-1-5127-6954-8 (e)

Library of Congress Control Number: 2016920871

Print information available on the last page.

WestBow Press rev. date: 1/16/2017

DEDICATION

To a precious friend, who happened to be my niece. Thank you for believing in me, this book, its message—and for the many talks we had about its contents. You prayed your heart out for me, encouraged me, and offered compassion and a shared understanding. I love you tons, more than I can express, and I miss you just as much. This book is for you, and for all others like us and the ones our stories will affect and have affected—our husbands, our children, our families, and others who have paid dearly for what was done to us and then what we suffered and did. May God redeem it all. I am praying our lives will impact many lives with the redemption Christ came to give. I dedicate my life, our stories, especially their disasters and fallouts to be messages of hope to the glory of God.

"For many in our high-paced world, despair is not a moment; it is a way of life."
--Ravi Zacharias, *Can Man Live Without God*

Yet, the LORD makes known to me the path of life; in His presence there
is fullness of joy; at His right hand are pleasures forevermore.
--Psalm 16:11, ESV (paraphrased)

FOREWORD

But God. We overcome because He overcame!

And they overcame and conquered him because of the blood of the Lamb and because of the word of their testimony, for they did not love their life and renounce their faith even when faced with death. (Revelation 12:11, AMP)

Covenant God... Hope against all hope. His mystery and power, His victory, Christ our hope (Genesis 12; Romans 4:18; John 19:30; 1 Timothy 1:1b).

Listen! I am telling you a mystery: Death has been swallowed up in victory.
Death, where is your victory?
Death, where is your sting?
Now the sting of death is sin,
and the power of sin is the law.
But thanks be to God, who gives us the victory
through our Lord Jesus Christ! (1 Corinthians 15:51, HCSB)

Praise be to the God and Father of our Lord Jesus Christ! In his great mercy He has given us new birth into a living hope through the resurrection of Jesus Christ from the dead. 1 Peter 1:3

We have eternal life now: John 17:3: Now this is eternal life: that they know you, the only true God, and Jesus Christ, whom you have sent.

The Lord is my chosen portion and my cup...
The lines have fallen for me in pleasant places;
indeed, I have a beautiful inheritance. (Psalm 16:5-6, ESV.)

We have hope eternally in our afterlife: In Christ our "names are written in heaven." (Luke 10:20, NIV).

In my Father's house are many rooms…I go and prepare a place for you, I will come again and will take you to myself, that where I am you may be also (John 14:2-3 ESV).

And the angel said to me, "Write this: Blessed are those who are invited to the marriage supper of the Lamb" (Revelation 19:9).

"Hope comes from the promises of God rooted in the work of Christ." John Piper

CONTENTS

INTRODUCTION
THE ELEPHANT IN THE ROOM

There is an elephant in the room. Too large for the space it inhabits, it's destroying its home from the inside out, crashing into mirrors and smashing into walls. Yet we usually don't talk about it. We act like it doesn't exist, though the damage persists and we find ourselves staring at it in hopelessness, wondering if we must deal with this forever, and alone.

Our elephants are our secrets, our secret sins, the ones we never mention. The things too shameful for us to say: things like sexual abuse, abortion, homosexuality, and addiction. In our culture, the elephants are the hot topics, sometimes used to bludgeon the church into silence even when Jesus would beckon us to take a righteous stand. Sometimes, if the church does take a stand and talk about the elephant, it still doesn't usually know how to help the people affected and bring them to restoration.

These elephants often wear masks to try to look more appealing, but they can't really hide. They're still elephants, and they're still in the room. If we leave the elephant masked, we run the risk of never again being free. We refuse to be honest with the facts of our story and where the secrets came from, whether in the church or on a personal level—and that's how an elephant in the room becomes a controlling skeleton in the closet.

I can no longer live the charade. Pretending does not work, and it hinders the Gospel. In *Sacred Secrets,* Beth Moore states, "Secrets manifest."[1]

In the DVD of this study, she states,

> *"Our triumphs and our defeats erupt from our vaults." What is vaulted in you is the seat of your success and failure, your triumphs and defeats. It is impacting and living itself out all over your life. That is what we have come to tend to. So much defeat is caught up in that vault. What I want to prove to you Scripturally is that every true success, every true Biblical success will come from that same vault. Right there in that secret place.[2]*

Psalm 51. Our secrets taken to the Lord, get redeemed.

Jesus knows all of our secrets. There are no secrets with Him. He knows all about us and loves us completely. He does not want us in secrecy, shame, or condemnation and has done everything to bring blessing and redemption through forgiveness that comes by His sacrifice.

I want to be genuine, so I will no longer hide or pretend. I have faced the truth and been to the cross, and I have appropriated Christ's work by faith. I have begun to live authentically and this is where I will unmask, taking off the old man, that skeleton of shame and disgrace I have worn or carried for so long and putting on the righteousness of Christ.

This book is my story of how the Gospel was first heralded to me and Christ became *life* to me. It is the story of how I began to herald, or share with others, what I have received.

REDEMPTION IN THE TELLING

Because I carried so much shame, initially it seemed impossible to write my story and apply the Gospel to it effectively. Shame robbed me, disconnecting me from the Gospel's power. I began trying to make the Gospel work by my "good works" instead. I thought that if I tried harder, I would find hope. I never found hope or peace or joy because I was locked in shame by default—and habit. Shame became my identity, and it affected my relationships and every part of my life. I craved relief from myself—from trying to prove my value because I felt worthless. If you met me, you'd think I was self-assured and confident, which I used as a defense. I needed a deeper experience of God's love and Christ's cross.

It is God's will for my story, all our stories, to be redeemed. In hearing mine, perhaps you will experience His story in a greater way. Perhaps you will gain insights and a greater grace understanding to apply to your story to bring redemption in a greater measure.

To herald the Gospel to the world more effectively, we must be sure we have embraced the love of God, know the Truth of God, and have discovered the secret of hope found in Him. This process begins with Christ's covenant story and our personal story.

It continues with our being able to have true confidence in Christ's story, knowing the elephants cannot trample us: accepting the truth of the Gospel and the need we have to herald it. Heralding the Gospel, both to ourselves and to others, is a vital step on our way to healing.

THROUGH THE GOSPEL LENS

As I began committing the truths of God's Word to my heart by writing and processing my past through the Gospel lens and the Spirit's work, the shame diminished more and more and the desire to share my story came through. My head knowledge is becoming heart functioning in Gospel living.

As one thinks in his heart so he is (Proverbs 23:7, NKJV).

Paul told us, "To live is Christ," and Jesus told Peter, "strengthen the brethren." Oh how wonderful if the Lord would work in us, me and you, and by His Spirit, teach us to live like these first apostles in the Book of Acts. We too could turn the world upside down with the Gospel!

Now I want to make clear for you, brothers and sisters, the Gospel that I preached to you, that you received and on which you stand, and by which you are being saved, if you hold firmly to the message I preached to you—unless you believed in vain. For I passed on to you as of first importance what I also received—that Christ died for our sins according to the scriptures, and that he was buried, and that he was raised on the third day according to the scriptures (1 Corinthians 15:3-4, NET).

WORK IN PROGRESS

I am a work in progress, and it's been messy. I am learning to accept myself and my past in the light of God's grace and truth. Religion, or a set of rules to follow based on our own works, doesn't work. But the experience of the true Gospel based on the sacrificial death of Christ has opened my eyes to hope. Resurrection hope.

I have received God's grace and mercy. Christ died to give me these unmerited favors. Though I received them in the past, at times I have poorly understood them and rarely applied their riches or utilized their gifts. Shame has hindered Christ's forgiveness too long. I was deceived to think I could overcome shame by my own works.

The realization of my dependence on works has been intense. I realized how much I depended on my performance to make me righteous. I continue to process my feelings and abide more fully in Christ. Only Christ's blood overcomes shame and all sin and brings the victory. "Without the shedding of blood there is no forgiveness of sins." (Hebrews 9:22, ESV.)

I want to use what I have learned from the Word and to live what it teaches and what I say I believe—and I want to share this process with you. Christ promises victory!

The process of breaking my silence and revealing my secrets as well as breaking out of legalistic religion has not been easy. It has been a slow kill inside of me. But in its death, new life has hope. I fully desire to overcome (Revelation 12:11), worship in Spirit and in truth (John 4:23-24), and live a life of abundance (John 10:10; Ephesians 3:20).

We are greatly loved and intimately known. The creator of the universe loves and cares about us, individually and specifically. His love is more than words and sentiment. His unconditional love is backed by action, the giving of His life. He knows us fully—our inner thoughts, feelings, and our outer actions, including every good or bad thing we have ever thought, said or have done. And yet He loves us. His love is infinite and is unaffected by our past.

His love gives us hope.

The Elephant Gospel is what happens when we acknowledge the elephant in the room and take off our masks to recognize our brokenness and bondage. Then we begin to herald the message of Jesus Christ as it was meant to be heralded: first, with honesty and genuineness to ourselves; second, through the Body of Christ to the hurting and broken world. The saying goes that an elephant never forgets. It is ours, through the Gospel, never to forget the hope that was won for us on the cross. The Elephant Gospel is the story of the secret of our hope.

And my hope for this book is that, as I take off my own mask and discuss the elephant herd that has touched my life, my secrets now told will show the secret of hope, as I have discovered it, to you. I am learning how to depend only on Christ to deliver me and take my old self to the cross, leaving it there for good. No longer may it have a negative hold on me. The stronghold of shame is broken. My identity in Christ is secure.

I pray the finish to my life will make the enemy very sorry he ever messed with me. Hope from hopelessness.

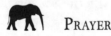 PRAYER

LORD, in the Holy Spirit and with much assurance in power and in word may our gospel come forth (1 Thessalonians 1:5). May the focus be on Christ and His completed redemptive work accomplished on our behalf. Give us clear words of testimony about how Christ's blood purchased salvation. Open the eyes of the unsaved so they may see the truth of how sin separates us from you. Thank you for grace for repentance and faith in Christ. Help us unmask the elephants through Christ's work for salvation, not depending on our own works. In Jesus' name, amen.

PART 1:
The Elephant Shackled

Circus elephants are magnificent creatures. They parade underneath the colorful big top, amidst the antics of the clowns, the tricks of the acrobats, and the smells of cotton candy and popcorn. The circus elephant lives to entertain and amaze. But perhaps the most amazing thing is that an enormous elephant can be kept in line by just a shackle attached to a tiny stake in the ground: a stake the elephant could easily overpower and be free from. But why doesn't it? Because the elephant was chained to that stake since its babyhood. It tried and tried throughout its young life to break free from that shackle, but it learned through hardship and struggle to see the stake as its master. Now, as a "well-adjusted adult," the elephant believes it cannot get free, and doesn't even try any longer.

When horrible things happen to us at a young age, shame tries to take over. Lies get entrenched and seem so true. Trusting in God's love seems impossible—we more easily trust in counterfeits. Horrible things are bad enough on their own, but Satan takes them and exploits them for his own advantage, to kill, steal, and destroy, deceiving us into thinking God doesn't love us. Just look at all these awful things that are happening to us, all the terrible things that we have done!

Shame becomes our chain, our stake, and we believe we can never escape. Sometimes it begins with things that are done to us, but often it continues with our own choices. Sometimes we choose hopelessness instead of hope.

At this stage in the journey of the Elephant Gospel, we may try to self-manage our sin by our works, say our sin is okay, or even parade it, pretending we feel no shame because it is easier to say we are not wrong than to admit we need to change. This elephant's Gospel needs a confrontation with Christ's death on the cross to truly find hope.

It is hard to imagine we could be capable of evil and then be deceived into thinking enough "goodness" would balance the scales. But this is the way I have lived without realizing it. As I give "the word of my testimony," my story, please remember that if you were given my life, you too could have done the things I have done.

My Story; An Elephant's Story

You will give birth to a son, and you are to give him the name Jesus,
because he will save his people from their sins (Matthew 1:21, KJV).

*Sin is the second most powerful force in the universe, for it sent Jesus to the
cross. Only one force is greater—the love of God."* --Billy Graham

*"Knowing God without knowing my own wretchedness makes for pride. Knowing my own
wretchedness without knowing God makes for despair. Knowing Jesus Christ strikes the
balance because he shows us both. God and our own wretchedness.* -- Blaise Pascal

He who did not spare his own Son but gave him up for us all, how will he
not also with him graciously give us all things. (Romans 8:32, ESV)

My Hopeless Story

When I was two and a half, neither my doctors nor my parents expected me to live.

I was severely ill with high fevers that brought on seizures, including the longest grand
mal seizure my doctor had seen to date. Initially I was diagnosed with encephalitis. After many
spinal taps, numerous shots, countless medications, and various tests in that intense time of
hospitalization, the doctors told my parents that if I recovered from this infection in my brain,
I may be mentally impaired or sustain other negative long-term effects.

The cause and diagnosis were never confirmed, but the after-effects were unpleasant: I
grew fast and looked, acted, and felt different than I did before. The doctors said they thought
the illness had affected my brain, growth, and possibly my cognition, though thankfully over

time the effects seemed to stabilize. Nevertheless, in my childhood I suffered from these abnormalities, and other children teased me.

THE BEGINNING OF ABUSE

I do not know when the sexual abuse started or when it stopped, but many of my earliest memories are sexual. I have no precise memories of this early abuse, but I have all the signs, feelings, and many "before-and-after scenes" that can be pieced together. Counselors see the clear signs of sexual abuse. I feel great shame. I have felt unlovable, defective and as though I do not belong. Not knowing why I feel what I feel or remembering the actual details of the abuse disturbs and haunts me.

Feeling abnormal, rejected, and unlovable has been a way of life from my earliest memories. These feelings led me to behave in unusual ways. My actions concerned my mother, and she took me to our family doctor when I was a preschooler to find out what was wrong with me. But in the early 1960s, symptoms of sexual abuse were not recognized and diagnosed as they are today. The doctor told my mom I would grow out of these behaviors.

I felt repeated shame and humiliation and confusion as my mother tried to help me grow out of these abnormal behaviors. I knew I wasn't normal, but I did not understand how to become "normal." I know now that my mom loved me, wanted to help me, and was doing all she knew to do. However, all I wanted then was to feel more of her love and acceptance. I just felt disgusting and disgraced. I tried to be good, because I thought if I was good enough I would be loved. Yet I still saw myself as unlovable and bad.

I lived with agonizing feelings of self-hatred and self-rejection. I got to the point that I was afraid to use the bathroom because I might touch myself and be dirty. This was my understanding as a preschooler. I remember wanting to die, even as early as five. I thought of drinking some of the weed killer or chemicals stored in the garage.

By about the age of six, many of the effects of the severe illness and abnormal behaviors had normalized, but my growth and a few disabilities continued to be problematic. I was very aware of how big I was and how concerned my parents were about it. I was also hyperactive with a few learning issues. It was not a good mix—to appear to be the oldest, yet be the youngest. It only accentuated the deficits. I was bigger and taller than my older siblings and all my classmates, and I felt awkward and out of place, even with my family and peers. I was treated like I was older than I was, but I couldn't meet the expectations of my presumed age, so I felt shamed. I tried my best to behave and was an obedient child to the best of my ability.

HINTS OF HOPE

Before I go on, I want to mention that there were stabilizing forces throughout my childhood, too.

I remember my dad holding me in his lap, saying, "You are my little girl," and I felt his love and affection. Every night, my mother would kiss me goodnight and pray with me. "Sweet dreams," she always told me. "I love you. God bless you." Also, I felt loved by my siblings.

To provide for us during the early years, Daddy sometimes worked three jobs. He was at work during much of my preschool years, so most of the responsibility to raise us fell to my mom. Mom did her best to keep things organized and consistent, and she ran our household well. As I look back on it now, I admire her and what she accomplished.

My parents were married more than fifty years and did their best to live their faith before us. They worked hard to provide for us, were orderly and clean, and set good examples of a healthy lifestyle. We had a moral, upstanding family.

We attended church faithfully. Every Sunday and all Christian holidays, my family was at church and often at catechism. My first Holy Communion and Confirmation were highlights of my childhood. I did not understand how God was with me always, or that I needed a Savior and why, but I had heard and knew about Jesus, and I knew He had died on a cross. Sadly, my conclusion as to His extraordinary sacrifice was that I needed to be good to please God and receive His love.

Despite the challenges I faced personally, I can see evidence of God's love and favor in my life. He gave me talents and abilities with extra measures of perseverance, persistence, motivation, and a willingness to work hard. These often accentuated the special gift of athleticism I have been privileged to possess and immensely enjoy. I am so thankful for these consistent stabilizing factors in my childhood.

ATTACKED

When I was four or five years old, I was held down on the ground by a mentally unstable neighbor. He had me fully pinned and was on top of me with his hand over my mouth and nose, which blocked my airway. I was petrified. I could not breathe. Thankfully my protective two older siblings and our mother came to my rescue just in time, before anything worse happened.

The man said things to me while he held me down. I do not know his specific words. I was too young to fully understand them. I do know the impression they left on me: I was disgusting, worthless, and he wished I was dead. The effect this had on me seemed to confirm my worst fears. I believed these impressions to be the truth. On top of that, I felt guilty. I was in his parents' yard, where my parents had forbidden me to go. I felt what happened was my fault.

I vowed to be more obedient and worthy of love. My focus and obsession worsened in trying to be good. Still I struggled to be still and quiet especially in school; because of my hyperactive tendencies, the doctor wanted to treat me with Ritalin™, a new drug. My parents didn't want to risk it, given my medical history.

LOOKING FOR LOVE

I have precise memories of a certain day when I was about nine years of age, of "before and after scenes" that are terrifying to me. As my counselor and I worked through these memories, I became convinced I was sexually abused in a very traumatic and unusual way by someone my parents thought they could trust. I think the man was drunk when the abuse occurred, and it was only a one-time event. But even once was too much. I developed a wrong concept of love, and it impacted how I interacted with boys my age. I thought that if a boy wanted to touch me, I was accepted and it was love. What a lie I believed!

Before I was twelve, I invited the boys in the neighborhood to meet me at the fort, telling them they could do whatever they wanted to do. To this day I wonder, *Why would I offer myself like that?* Nobody came. Nobody came! I determined that I was unlovable and unwanted. I walked around in the woods wanting to die. I was too afraid to talk to anybody about these fears and thoughts. I blamed myself and did not know what to do to be better.

When my art teacher told us to draw a picture of who we wanted to be, I tried to draw my sister. I thought, *Maybe if I could be a different girl, things would be better.* In my mind, she was far superior—prettier and more feminine. I was much bigger than everyone in my class until 6th grade, when one of the other students finally attained my height. I was strong, but often clumsy; my fine motor skills had not developed. Although I tried to be more coordinated, I was often told I was a "bull in a china shop." It hurt. I acted as though it didn't. I felt weak, but I pretended to be strong. There was safety in strength. I didn't know how to be like other girls.

So I became a full-fledged tomboy, and got in trouble many times for playing football and doing things only boys were supposed to do, even though I was better at sports than many of the boys in our neighborhood. I was a talented athlete—the one thing I loved about myself. The only times I really liked me were when I performed well in sports. For the most part, though, I hated being me and wanted out of my body.

I never felt good enough and tirelessly strived to be better, different—whatever would get me to feel loved, whether I was loved or not, if I just could feel loved for that moment. It was a formula that led me into much trauma, abuse, sin, and sadness. I just wanted to be okay with who I was, and I wanted others to be okay with me, too.

The kids in my neighborhood teased me for my size and even my ethnicity—my father's family were full-fledged immigrants. Thankfully we moved far from that neighborhood about the time I entered my teens. In the new neighborhood, I was accepted.

I continued to have a great ability in sports, and coaches esteemed me. I learned to work radically to make the most of these talents, and the acceptance that came with this spurred me onward. Sports became my life. I swam competitively on a national team and practiced for hours most days from the age of 12 until I was about 18 years old. One coach encouraged me to try for the Olympics. Although I did not make it to the international stage, swimming was a stabilizing factor in my life. Athleticism was the one area of my life where I felt successful and valued.

Then in my late teens, my spinal health deteriorated (due to a defect I was born with). I was unable to continue swimming at that level of competition. My life fell apart. I had lost the identity I found in the value I had in my performance.

HEARING ABOUT HOPE

My conclusions about life were that I could be right with God just by going to church and being good. During a youth retreat on the July Fourth weekend when I was fourteen, I heard the Gospel for the first time: I learned I was a sinner, that I had to accept Christ's gift on the cross, and ask forgiveness for my sins in order to be restored to my heavenly Father and be saved.

At the retreat, I heard a lot of the others' testimonies, telling about all the bad things they had done—drinking, smoking pot, partying hard. They made their partying sound so fun I wondered if they regretted giving up something that had been so pleasurable for them. I was confused. What had they gained? Well, I hadn't done any of those "bad" things—I'd never used drugs or alcohol because of my commitment to swimming—so I felt pretty good about myself in comparison! However, I had lied and cheated in school, had hate in my heart, and I often felt dirty, defiled, and bad. I was convicted of my sin and did not want to go to hell, so I said the sinner's prayer, and I felt peace in my heart.

Just weeks after my salvation experience, I was taken to a party by a trusted adult relative. I had no idea what that night would usher into my life. I did not know that it would be an occult party, and that abuse would take place. The years that followed were undoubtedly the worst in my life. My life after the occult abuse unraveled at a rapid pace and in an awful way. From the age of fifteen to twenty-one, I lived in depravity. I embraced sin. I regret those years more than any in my life, and I can't explain the force that drove me. It felt as if I was under some curse or spell that I could not break.

All semblance of normalcy in my core identity was attacked repeatedly. The innocence I wanted to live was adulterated by perversion. The enemy capitalized on the foundational lies of my early childhood. The monsters of fear, insecurity, betrayal, counterfeit love, worthlessness, and sexual sins consumed me.

BETRAYAL, CONFUSION, COLLAPSE

My two first serious boyfriends, whom I had trusted, betrayed me. I thought it was my new commitment to purity and my fear of sex that caused both of them to ultimately reject me. I desperately wanted to know I was wanted, but I held back, giving mixed messages of desire and restraint. I was trying to be a good Christian girl, but I was a mess, a tease, a contradiction, and mass of confusion.

I talked to a close girlfriend about my fears and insecurities related to sex and boys. In the sharing, we got too close. Our talks turned into the worst nightmare of my life. For about a year, I was sexually confused, searching to make sense of life and my identity. Shame defined me.

When I went away to college, I carried the secret, the shame, and the confusion, hiding my struggle from everyone. I tried to seek God. I made a decision to never go "that way" again—a resolution I have always kept. My "friendship" with the other girl ended completely.

I believed that if I told my parents or my church, I would be cast out and disowned. I would have no home and no support, and no one would understand. So I kept it to myself, and I felt so alone. In the 1970s, homosexuality was still designated a mental illness. Even though by the late 70's culture was beginning to consider homosexuality differently, I still thought it was considered by most to be a blight and a terrible affliction, a stigma, an abnormality, and completely unacceptable. "Completely unacceptable": that description fit how I often felt much of my young life.

I wanted to turn back time for a do-over, but that's never possible, is it? I was more confused than ever, and I was still afraid of men. Once again, I prided myself on how strong I could be, and I hid behind the false strength.

Like a roller coaster, my mess of emotions careened to wild ups and downs. I struggled with an eating disorder, and like most college kids, I used alcohol. I discovered that partying wasn't the pleasure others had seemed to present it to be. It never brought lasting joy; and for me, it created more problems and hurt than any minimal pleasure it gave. Alcohol and pain were a bad mix for me. Too often my pain and emotions came out when I drank. Eventually,

I saw that alcohol was a problem in my life, so I tried to clean up my act and I basically quit drinking altogether.

Loved at Last

My third year of college, I met the "stand-out" man who is now my husband of more than 35 years. I thought he was the best thing that ever happened to me. He wrote me love poems and notes, and called me a special nickname. I fell deeply in love with him, and I cherished the thoughts of his heart. I finally felt treasured and loved! We had a very romantic first year together.

I trusted him, and I shared my heart with him as well as my body. I even told him my teenage secret—he was the only person who knew. But he accepted me, and assured me of his love and my value. I thought my life could finally be different and better.

We were both believers, but obviously not pure—it was no secret that we were involved. I was a bad witness to our families and friends saying I was Christian, but living in sexual intimacy outside of marriage. To me, it was almost a stamp of approval that said, "See? A man wants me." I had no idea how distorted my perverted thinking was.

My then-boyfriend and I spoke of our belief in God—both of us desired to grow closer to Him. We planned to have a large family together—six to eight children. But I have to admit, I had fears about marriage. I was afraid to vulnerably trust any man. I prayed about whether I should marry him, and I felt that He was God's choice for me. I remember the day he asked for my father's permission to marry me. My father and my family loved (and love) him, accepted him with open arms, and gave us unanimous approval. We were engaged a short time and married a little over a year after first meeting. He was safe and loving, and I trusted him.

D-Day

Months after we married, I unexpectedly got pregnant. To my shock and utter horror, he did not want this unplanned pregnancy. I saw this as our baby; at the time, he saw it as an accident, an untimely mistake we could not afford.

I begged and cried to keep the pregnancy. I desperately wanted our baby. I wanted my husband too, but I felt the only way to keep him was to do as he desired. I had such turmoil about who I was and my value; and sadly, my husband's opinion of me was my barometer. I did not realize at the time that the loss of our baby would spell out my loss of my husband and of myself as well. Our choice became a breeding ground for death.

I was also afraid my secrets would be exposed. No one knew about my teenage relationship.

I had not sought any treatment for my eating disorder, and it seemed to control my life. I felt ill-equipped to be a mom—too unstable even to care for myself and our marriage.

Since it was only a few days past my period when the pregnancy was confirmed, I told myself it was just like birth control. *Only cells; the heart was not formed.*

The day we aborted our first child was a D-day for us. It has defined and destroyed many of our days and much of my life. I felt our life and family was constantly missing an important person—our child.

I was not the same afterward. I couldn't stop thinking about the baby and the abortion. The more I tried to put it out of my mind, the more the memories chased me. And the more I suffered, the more I blamed my husband and myself.

Our marriage was in shambles, and our great loss became greater. We were becoming enemies to each other, distrusting, sad, and no longer very loving. Unforgiveness and bitterness threatened to destroy me, us. I lived by rote, my heart grieved, dead, and buried by the ashes, pain, betrayals, and agony. The rejections of my young years repeated themselves.

The skeleton in the closet of my soul had not just controlled me, but it had become the poison that was killing me little by little, piece by piece. I needed an extraction and a resurrection.

For years I struggled with suicidal thoughts, fighting to keep sane, in horror that others might someday find out. I can honestly say if I had not sought Christ during this time, I would not be alive today.

The mask of performance I hid behind came naturally to me. My life seemed normal for the most part. However, there was no mistaking the volcano that sometimes erupted in me, which surely affected my family as well.

I have suffered more than thirty years grieving this deadly and awful decision, and have struggled against unforgiveness and bitterness. I should have refused the abortion and done whatever I needed to do to keep the pregnancy. Part of the consequence was the death I felt inside. I knew my past sin, and how I longed so deeply for love and acceptance from a man. I felt unlovable.

There are times I am mad at God for allowing me to suffer and go through such horror. I prayed about marrying my husband. Was I fooled into thinking it was God's will when it wasn't? Why did all this have to happen? Why could it not have been prevented? It has taken the supernatural intervention of God for us to live the Gospel, receiving forgiveness, forgiving ourselves and each other through Christ, and choosing to continue to love.

In these forty-plus years since my older teen years of sexual sins and the more than thirty years since our abortion, I have lived with that mask on, trying to pretend all of this never happened. I did not think I would ever tell these secrets or give this kind of personal testimony.

At various times during my marriage and our family life, I felt I had reached rock bottom. Like a circus elephant, I had accepted bondage as normal, seeing no other way of life, wearing my colorful mask as if everything was okay. I didn't know I could be free, how to get free, or how to live free. Defining and finding the key to unlock all shackles and reconditioning my thinking has been a process for me, a process in the midst of hopelessness. And it started with taking off the mask and being honest with my weakness.

Perhaps your story, too, contains elephants, shackles, and skeletons. Maybe your story shares similarities with the elephant's tale. My hope is to help us look at our shackles, secrets, what has held us back, and what has poisoned our thinking and our souls. Then we can begin to apply the truths that will free us and help us be restored. Our stories do not always start out great, but they can still be great, the bad turned to good. There is a time to look back and learn and there is a time to go forward in freedom with what you learned. The time for healing is now.

 PRAYER

LORD, I don't even know how to pray right now. It is so hard to share and admit how sinfully and hopelessly I have lived. Thank you that you know all about what we have done, but you still love us so completely. Please help people who have experienced any of these things to know they too can live free and be forgiven and healed, with a clear conscience in Christ. Please help us receive the gift of forgiveness that you have extended to us so freely and completely; may we experience the Gospel's power to transform and then extend it to others. Please help us all to live, despite our circumstances, welcoming the message with joy from the Holy Spirit (1 Thessalonians 1:6). Help us to live in your hope, your Gospel. In Jesus' name, amen.

THE WORLD NEEDS HOPE

*Once you were alienated and hostile in your minds because of your evil actions.
But now He has reconciled you by His physical body through His death, to present
you holy, faultless, and blameless before Him. (Colossians 1:21-22, HCSB)*

*"The truth is, God doesn't grade on a curve; he grades on a cross… A grace
economy is backward to most of us—those who think they qualify, don't;
and those who admit they don't qualify, do." Jefferson Bethke[3]*

*John 4:10, MSG: Jesus answered, "If you knew the generosity of God (gift of God, KJV) and
who I am, you would be asking me for a drink, and I would give you fresh, living water."*

Grace is but glory begun, and glory is but grace perfected. Jonathan Edwards

Yesterday, we buried my niece. Her life was filled with tragedies. She was just two years old
when abuse began by an older boy, a distant relative. Nobody suspected him. Her family
thought they could trust them to play together at gatherings. He not only thought of hurting
her, but continued to hurt her sexually and emotionally for years. She struggled to believe
God loved her and struggled to love herself.

My niece became a special friend to me, someone who understood me in a way few do.
We were close; we had some things from our early years in common. But our responses to
those years were radically different. For some years, heroin, cocaine, and alcohol were her
life-sustaining, pain-deadening mainstays.

God's grace and love showed throughout her life, but as her life progressed this seemed
to pour out in immense ways. She had chance after chance after chance to live new. The lies
that she believed, however, acted as barriers to her receiving from God and breaking free.

God forgave all of her sins. She knew she had received forgiveness for great sin, but the sins against her and the lies they fueled were so hard to overcome, she could not consistently hear and respond to the calls of God's love and grace that beckoned her. The torment was real; the battle raged fiercely, brutally, relentlessly.

Elephants, shackles, and skeletons often come from these places of despair and victimization. The shackled-elephant life is a toxic life of bondage, isolation, and limitation that tragically sometimes results in death.

The elephant in the room of our life can leave a skeleton in our soul. If it remains untouched, unhealed, and undealt with, it can be every bit as toxic as poison to our wellbeing.

I have experienced this firsthand. My own life story interfaces with four major issues of our times:

- Sexual abuse and exploitation of children
- Marred distinction between genders, homosexuality, and gender confusion
- Abortion
- Judgment and condemnation from the church

And it's not just my story; there are many like me, like us. This is our world. In a recent radio broadcast, host Janet Parshall interviewed two authors, Juli Slattery and Linda Dillow, and featured their book *Surprised by the Healer*. In that interview, the authors said that one in three girls and one in six boys are sexually abused before the age of eighteen. The estimates are that 60 million survivors of childhood sexual abuse are in America today and approximately two thirds of US men view pornography at least monthly, including Christian men, who virtually mirror the national average. Janet mentioned that every line was lit as phone calls poured in during the entire show.

There are more than 53 million women (and with the men involved, more than 100 million people total) who have made the choice to abort their children in America. The womb—though meant to be a safe haven—has become a tomb, a holocaust site. There are multitudes of boys, girls, men, and women who have gone into homosexuality or bisexuality, and even more who still deal with the trauma of abuse they suffered as children. Suicide, addiction, and health issues have escalated astronomically.

If you identify with the shackled elephant, you are certainly not alone.

WE ARE AT WAR

We are at war. Foundational biblical truths are being attacked. Satan is working relentlessly to deceive us into thinking God's love is not pure, perfect, or good. He attempts to diminish our love and fervor for God and His Gospel. We are told in 2 Corinthians 11:3 (ESV), "But I am afraid that as the serpent deceived Eve by his cunning, your thoughts will be led astray from a sincere and pure devotion to Christ." This is Satan's way from the beginning. He works every possible device to counter the love and faithfulness of God.

Today Satan's bullseyes could be said to be the cross and work of Christ. The cross of Christ is the greatest gift of love, the greatest demonstration of God's love in existence. There is no place Satan works his evil more intensely than to get us to dismiss and discount this place of death, the cross, that is the seedbed of love, life and hope for us!

Satan tries to block our understanding, experience, and perception of God's love for us. This love is most dramatically expressed through the cross. Satan wounds our souls, sowing lies through sins committed to us or by us. These lies can cloud and can distort who God is and what He has done, is doing, and will do to show His love. These lies affect our hope and thus our love for God.

The Godhead and His work of redemption and love are constantly under attack by the enemy. We all need to be aware of the extent and power of this attack in our daily lives, and be on the defensive to block Satan's advances. To fail to be aware is to allow Satan to rob us of the truth, giving him access to wreak havoc in an attempt to destroy the plan and purpose God has for us.

THE GRUESOME FACTS

Reality is tragic… and it isn't pretty. I am going to write a brief section here that is raw and ugly, but poignant—and maybe you'd rather not read it. You can skip ahead to "The Woman at the Well," and know that we won't dwell on the carnage.

A popular recent movie, *Lincoln,* contains graphic war images—bodies strewn on top of one another, blood flowing in dark red trails to a dump where even more bodies are heaped in a pile. As Lincoln solemnly surveys the scene he is passed by a soldier wheeling a wheelbarrow of bloodied amputated limbs. It's sickening and nauseating, and it makes us cringe as we experience a reality of the horror of war and death and its aftermath. Some things can seem worse than death. But we rarely want to discuss or consider the gruesome nature of our own culture. It makes us uncomfortable. We usually don't want to go there. But isn't it necessary, in order to stop the carnage and its consequences?

Consider the shocking 2010 case of Dr. Kermit Gosnell, who was charged along with some of his employees with eight counts of murder and twenty-four counts of illegal late-term abortions. In his Pennsylvania "state-regulated" abortion clinic (a clinic of horrors) were discovered amputated baby feet in jars and other unbelievable atrocities. One reporter commented that Kermit Gosnell did what he did because people looked the other way. It's up to us to make sure history doesn't repeat itself. [4]

When I was about six months pregnant and on duty as an obstetrics nurse, I cared for a baby who almost survived a late-term abortion. As I cared for that child, I was thankful my own baby was safe inside my womb. However, I was forced to face the horror of my own abortion, which had happened five years earlier. My husband and I had contributed to the holocaust against the unborn. Both abortion experiences rocked my world forever and instilled in me a passion for life and a ferocity and audacity to stand against the Gosnells of this world!

The number of people that died during the atrocities of the second World War are staggering. During the Nazi Holocaust more than 12,000 people were killed each day. Most would think that the average daily loss of life was the greatest in human history! In comparison though reports today set the daily abortion rate at more than ten times that—120,000-130,000 babies are murdered every day. How do we look the other way?

Other statistics are just as horrifying. According to a *JAMA* review of literature regarding the sexual abuse of boys, only 10 - 33% of male abuse victims ever tell anyone about the abuse. The review also found that, "Abused [male] adolescents, particularly those victimized by males, were up to 7 times more likely to self-identify as gay or bisexual than peers who had not been abused."[5]

Then we consider sex trafficking, a global, modern form of slavery in which traffickers use "violence, threats, lies, debt bondage, and other forms of coercion to compel adults and children to engage in commercial sex acts against their will."[6]

According to the Polaris Project, "The International Labor Organization estimates that there are 4.5 million people trapped in forced sexual exploitation globally," and "In a 2014 report, the Urban Institute estimated that the underground sex economy ranged from $39.9 million in Denver, Colorado, to $290 million in Atlanta, Georgia."[7]

We see figurative shackles—and we see literal ones. And all of them can be taken to the foot of the cross.

The cross was a place of agonizing suffering and pain. Christ had endured physical injury, beating to the point of unrecognition, nails through His hands and feet, a horrendous death—the cup of wrath meant for me, for you, for us—that is the fact that gives us hope. The fact that Jesus was willing to accept the cup of wrath for the judgment of sin, including my own, drops me to my knees. It is the basis upon which our hope is built. Terrible, awful, really bad things are nailed to the cross, and Christ takes the judgment for those things on our behalf when we place our faith in Him.

The cross's radically hideous nature is what brings us glorious hope—and I cannot neglect to mention that oh so often, ugliness precedes beauty. There is a price to be paid for the removal of our shackles, the payment of our sins, the exchange of death to life, the restoration of our fellowship, the fulfillment of our destinies.... Christ paid it all!

THE WOMAN AT THE WELL

If ever there was someone living a shackled-elephant life, it was the Samaritan woman Jesus met at the well in John 4. She had lived an immoral life for such a long time, she no longer even thought she could escape. Husband after husband, then living with a man to whom she wasn't married. She was looking for love in the wrong places and in the wrong ways. How hopeless that must have seemed! Not so unlike me.

But then... Jesus.

Jesus showed grace, mercy, acceptance, and honor to the woman at the well. He was a friend of sinners and did not condemn or look down on her. His style is to bring people to the truth, to be freed through truth and repentance. He spoke words of knowledge to her with such grace and love that the Samaritan woman boasted, "He told me everything I ever did!" Imagine her many sins, which she'd tried to hide, but now openly proclaimed. Jesus delights in mercy, not judgment. He had come to take her judgment. He valued her, revealing Himself as Messiah. He had come to die for her sins to save her from them. Mercy would be realized.

Jesus lived and modeled love for every race, gender, and sinner. Since He is perfect and sinless, He is good—for He truly is God incarnate. He came to earth to save us, lift us up, and release us from what holds us down: sin. Jesus is not the story book prince that saves one damsel. He is the King of Kings, God incarnate, that came to save us *all* from our sins, defeat death, and make eternal life possible for *any* who will believe and receive!

The Lord used John 4 and the interaction Jesus had with the woman at the well to help me understand that He knows all about me—He has seen all of me, all my life. He died in my place and forgave me completely, so like the woman at the well, I want to tell everyone how good Jesus is! He knows me fully, loves me perfectly, accepts me completely, believes in me unashamedly! Wow, what a Savior!

He is the restorer of our hope.

ASKING THE HARD QUESTIONS

As we consider our world and the great need for Jesus, let's ask some tough questions that may test our beliefs in the truth of God's Word. Please promise not to make quick judgments or stop reading just because of the questions. They are hard questions for a determined purpose. We'll address these questions, at least generally, in the words of this book and the other resources offered. But for now, base your answers on God's Word, not culture.

1. Do you believe God is fair, good, powerful, and able to do the impossible?
2. What is the reason a person can go to heaven? Can just anyone get there?
3. How can a person have assurance that they have eternal life?
4. Do you believe you are a good person? Will you go to heaven based on your goodness? Why or why not?
5. Would a good God send a good person to hell?
6. Do you believe a person can be a Christian and be homosexual and continue in this lifestyle long-term without any conviction? Why or why not?
7. Do you believe God forgives murderers? Pedophiles? Homosexuals? Transgenders? Parents who abort or abuse their children? Rapists? Pimps? Sex traffickers and sexually immoral individuals?
8. Can God transform people like these into fully functional, healthy people with an identity in Christ? Can these people go to heaven?
9. Do you believe heaven is for any person, even bad ones such as cheaters, thieves, liars, adulterers, gluttons, alcoholics, drug addicts, gamblers, idolaters, or any of the categories listed above, and/or those who lack compassion or love for others and/or Christ if they truly repent and believe in Christ?
10. Can your worst sin be used for good?

BEYOND ALL HOPE?

Satan works overtime to make sure we know we fall short of the purpose for which we were created. He uses that against us. Through his attacks and lies, Satan attempts to hinder us from fully understanding the Gospel or heralding it to ourselves and the world. A lot of people would have said I was beyond hope. I thought I was beyond hope. A lot of people feel like they're beyond hope. Remember, this is the way the enemy works to create thinking that we are all beyond hope of the Gospel.

God has given us the fireworks of John 4. He told this woman that everyone else had given up on believing that He was the Messiah. However, He hadn't given up on her. We think all people like her are too far gone, but in God's eyes, they're not too far gone! There is still hope! Christians need to understand this because when we don't, we don't herald the Gospel as we should.

The world likes to believe that the Gospel is offensive. People are offended when people who have been horrible end up with assurance of salvation, and "decent, moral" people don't. They do not understand the darkness of sin and the magnitude of sin's offense against a Holy God. We have all fallen short. We are all spiritually dead before receiving Christ. We need connected to God through the forgiveness of our sins. So when we understand what Christ did, that it's based on a God who took our sin upon himself, we know His death paid for our sin! It is Christ's gracious yet costly payment, His goodness and favor, the gift of God. So how can man be offended at His merciful gift? It should melt the offense away, but man's pride often interferes.

THE DAYS OF NOAH

The future days promised will be like the days of Noah (Matthew 24:37; Luke 17:26). We are to invite, tell, and warn people. It is their choice whether they come to the cross of Christ to be saved. The work of Christ makes available the Mercy Seat, where mercy triumphs over judgment for any who will believe.

Beware of those that are enemies of the cross of Christ, of Truth. Changing absolute truth to meet our individual slants and desires is too often designated "cultural truth."

Did you know there is actually a version of a Bible titled *The Queen James Bible*? It attempts to edit the Word of God and avoid saying that homosexuality is wrong. Many have worked hard to change the interpretation of the Bible to justify their lifestyles of sin, trying to say God approves. We must know the truth of God's Word and have our lives reflect it. As Christians, we evaluate our beliefs based on the Word of God, not our experiences, the culture, or our peers. We must examine our beliefs for any sign of lies. We need to know if our beliefs mix a version of the truth with false doctrine. If the Bible is not our standard of truth, we could ride on the flow of the culture or our peers—into deception and away from Gospel life and hope.

LIFE TRANSFORMATION

Accepting the Bible as absolute truth transformed my life because the unconditional love of God in the redemption of man is so counter-cultural, counter-human nature. Thankfully, it is God's nature. God is love. His true love is defined by His blood and sacrifice once and for all, for all of us that will believe. It is what Paul and Peter and the Great Awakening revivalists discovered. It is the secret or mystery of Christ: His New Covenant, our hope.

At the fall, man exchanged God's dominion for the enemy's authority. At the cross Christ made the way for the reversal and the return of God's dominion in man to be recovered, restored, redeemed. His resurrection power secured His Holy Spirit's indwelling presence for those who believe, are born again, and are translated into the Kingdom of Light: restored to the family of God. As we turn from our iniquities and turn to God through Christ for the forgiveness of our sins, and to be born of His Spirit, we are blessed. We must have a heart change, born from above, through the experience of Christ to be truly born of God. (John 3.)

Christ's central message—the one He preached and taught the disciples to teach—was to repent, for the Kingdom of Heaven is at hand (See Matthew 3:2, 4:17; Mark 1:14-15; Luke 5:32, 9:2, 24:47.) He sent His disciples out to live His Gospel and advance His Kingdom. He wants born-again believers—current-day disciples. When we appreciate and value our salvation, we want to live it out and herald the Gospel to bring this great salvation to the world—to rescue the perishing, the lost, the dying, the spiritually dead.

Each of us is given various talents and a call. When we answer the call and use our talents, we will someday hear the words, "Well done, good and faithful servant; you were faithful over a few things, I will make you ruler over many things. enter into the joy of your lord. …Then the King will say to those on his right hand, 'Come, ye blessed of my Father, inherit the kingdom prepared for you from the foundation of the world. …Verily I say unto you, inasmuch as ye have done *it* unto one of the least of these my brethren, ye have done it unto me" (from Matthew 25:23, 34, 40, NKJV).

Jesus is the only answer to our stories of hopelessness. In fact, He is the mystery, the secret of hope. (Colossians 1, 1 Timothy 3:16; Phil 2-3.)

THE NEED IS GREAT

My niece and I both struggled so deeply to believe in God's love and to love and accept ourselves. With her passing, I began to search for answers. The most profound one came from a question: Why do I love God? Simply put, because He first loved me (1 John 4:19). Because of His proven, perfect love, forgiveness, and offer of salvation at the great cost of His Son at the cross. Christ gave Himself so I could experience the incredible gift of being known and accepted just as I am for who I am. He proved my value and worth to Him by His death and resurrection while I was still in my sin! Amazing love.

The more I have understood the cross, the more I have felt God's love, and the more I have begun to love myself. It became clear to me how relentlessly Satan works to thwart us, waylay us, and disconnect us from Christ! It is like having electricity in a house, but being convinced that doing life with no power source is best. So instead of using the light switch, we light candles and fight to keep them lit! The electric power is there all along, but we are not connected! This "big disconnect" is one of Satan's biggest strategies. We must never be disconnected from Christ and the cross, or the resurrection power is not accessed; it is disconnected or "in the off position" by our own choice to separate from Christ, the Preeminent Source. His Presence is Resurrection Power. Paul's number-one focus was Christ and Christ crucified; a life of power resulted. Resurrection power comes from Christ crucified life. This is the life of the secret of hope.

God did break through to my niece. She heard the truth and received Christ. She had five consecutive months with us prior to her homegoing. During that time, she reconciled with her mother, and seemed to believe conclusively that her mother and I and all our family and friends truly loved her. I think she also started to believe God loved her too, though she still seemed uncertain at times. She stated many evidences of faith, but she voiced questions about why God did not seem to answer so many of her prayers and why it was so hard to do the right thing. But she did live sober, and she was making strides. She died in more success than failure.

Her mother calls her "my precious daughter who taught me how to love." How could one that did not feel loved be so loving? But she was. And why did she not feel loved when so many loved her so much? Her loving so well, to me, is evidence of God's love and grace.

Our last conversation was very lengthy, most of a morning. I had been writing about the shackled elephant and shared the principles with her. I shared that we both needed to learn how to more effectively live the truth of what God says and not what we feel and what people have treated us like. I felt like our hearts connected and cried together in a deep way. It was staggering to me that this was my last conversation with her and it was about the shackled elephant that we both lived out in life so fully but needed to be free of so completely! I have thought about this often and it has spurred me on to want to make a difference for others like us before it is too late. I shared the way to get free and be free with her in detail through the Gospel and much of the writing of the book. I also was trying to share my theology in the ideas of the movie the Matrix and how the main character, Neo took the red pill. I shared about the red pill in my theological understanding of how most Christians are still living "in the pod of the world unaware" of what is really going on. How God has awakened me to a new and heightened level and that He is awakening many. He is bringing us "out" through an understanding of His full redemption by the blood of Christ. I tried my best to make sure she really understood the Gospel is about what Christ has done for her as she had expressed some conflicting thoughts. I said, "it is like taking that red pill. It is receiving what Christ did." Then

I asked her "If you could take a pill that would take away all shame, guilt, and all the wrong you have ever done, and give you a new heart and a new life, would you do it?" She said "Yes!" and I said, "That pill is the Gospel." That last conversation gives me such great hope that I will see her again in heaven. God is good and faithful and she received of him. That is Good News. It is the same for me and for all people. We all need to be spiritually made alive. We are spiritually disconnected from God until we come through Christ's red blood atonement.

My niece did believe in Jesus for the forgiveness of her sins. She did have the hope of Christ, what is more, Jesus surely goes ahead and prepares a place *"in His Father's house"* for His own. "The death of one that belongs to him is precious to the Lord" (Psalm 116:15, ICB). I believe she belonged to Him.

God knows our hearts and knows what blocks us from receiving Him more fully and has mercy. He knows the depths of hearts and the depths of the pain in our hearts; the torment and torture some have gone through is enormous. He died to free us, not condemn us. Truth sets us free.

What We Have in Common

Stories like my niece's, like mine, like the Samaritan woman's, are common in our world. Each person is searching for hope. Jesus declared that He is the answer to their search (John 14:6). Yet in our churches and in our lives, we often water down the message of salvation and try to make it about what we do and say. We act as if there were some big scale for God to weigh the good against the bad. If we try real hard, the scale will tip in the direction of the good and we will be saved. Our obedience does show our love for God, but it does not earn our salvation.

We must not hide the secret of hope. We must tell the world that Jesus died to pay our debt, and He offers salvation to anyone. Without Him, this world will be lost.

 Prayer

LORD, thank you that there is no greater love than what you accomplished on the cross. Our world has fallen so far short of your standards. Teach us to recognize our depravity. Help us put our faith in God and ring the LORD's message out (1 Thessalonians 1:8). Cause us to experience Christ, His cross and blood and new birth afresh. Help us be bold with the Gospel, for it is the power of God to salvation for any who will believe. Give us new encounters that will help us help others as we share the Gospel and lead others in love to the cross, where eternal life is offered through Christ. In Jesus' name, amen.

THE SECRET OF HOPE

For one will scarcely die for a righteous person—though perhaps for a good person one would dare even to die— but God shows his love for us in that while we were still sinners, Christ died for us. (Romans 8:7-8, ESV)

God's mercy and grace give me hope—for myself, and for our world.
~Billy Graham

It is by grace you have been saved, through faith—and this is not from yourself, it is a gift of God. (Ephesians 2:8, NIV)

The Gospel is "believe, saved, obey." Not that I obey, and therefore I am accepted; but that I am accepted in Jesus Christ and therefore I obey! Not "believe, obey, saved"; but believe, saved, obey! –Tim Keller, "Centrality of the Gospel" (See Appendix)

In the divine Scriptures, there are shallows and there are deeps; shallows where the lamb may wade, and deeps where the elephant may swim.
John Owen

At a lockdown facility for troubled youth, a rough-looking older teen approached me and the Director of Youth for Christ. Although he looked tough, his intense sad eyes were filled with tears as he told about a letter he received. "My Christian aunt wrote me," he said. "She says I am no good, and that I'm a black sheep that will never be a part of the family. That I am too bad to be reformed." Then he asked, "Do you think it's true? Is there any hope for me?"

My heart ached for him. His pain was palpable, but I felt paralyzed. I longed to help him, but as we talked my words were empty, and I could find nothing of real assurance to tell him.

It hit too close to home: I had also felt the shame, anger, despair, and desperation that I sensed in him.

Most of us have. This shame is the shackle that holds us in place. It is what causes us to lose hope of ever being free.

Sadly, even after all my years in the Word and my training as a Youth for Christ leader, I did not, at that time, know how to effectively give the Good News to this youth. Nor was I fully living it.

I had worked so hard to be better. Yet I lived in a performance-based religion that had me numbed, and I didn't understand cross-centered grace. I tried to prove my own value instead. Yet I did not realize that my works-based religion had me shackled. My level of understanding of the true Gospel was weak, and while I tried to share Christ's love for him, I do not think I shared the Gospel fully or clearly. Truth is, I was not living in its fullness. I was living a "Galatians Gospel" (my name for the works-based Gospel Paul warned the Galatians against) inside the true and real Gospel. I was saved but was living by the law and not depending on the Spirit of God or the empowerment of His grace.

I have thought of this young man often. My heart's desire and my prayer to God for him and youth like him, is for salvation and for understanding of the true Gospel. Like him, we can think we are too far gone to be good enough for God or like his aunt, we can think we are right with God because of our own goodness. The true Gospel is the message of God's goodness—not ours.

HOPE LIVES, EVEN HERE

For a time, darkness, sin, and death were winning in my life. "But God, being rich in mercy, because of the great love with which he loved us, even when we were dead in our trespasses, made us alive together with Christ — by grace you have been saved" (Ephesians 2:4–5, 8).

In the Gospel story, Christ the Son of God took on the darkness of sin: its shame, its curse, its wages, and ultimately death and hell to bring us forgiveness, light, grace, blessing, and ultimately new spiritual life, the gift of God, eternal life. His death brought us great salvation. Christ is the light that overcame the darkness of sin when He was resurrected from darkness and death. Nothing could hold Him down.

Those of us who know our shackles all too well know also the chasm we sense between ourselves and grace. Between ourselves and the mercy seat. Between ourselves and hope. I needed to break through from law to Gospel—from performance to grace! From myself and my hopelessness to hope in my God.

Surely we are too far gone! No matter how hard we try to leap from one side to another, we will always fall short (Romans 3:23). But that Gospel we keep mentioning tells us of the true bridge. Christ's cross, His death is the only thing that can fill the gap and build a bridge that allows us to reach the hope of salvation and forgiveness. Nothing else will satisfy. The Lord made it this way on purpose, so that no one can boast that he or she achieved salvation by any good works (Ephesians 2:8-9). It's only the cross that allows us access to God through Christ.

We'll return to the topic of the Gospel and what it truly is. But for now, just remember—because of Jesus' unconditional love and great sacrifice on your behalf there is hope for any who will believe.

OPERATION RESURRECTION

Christ overcame sin and death. Christ gives us His life, through the Holy Spirit who enters us. We are made new. Then we can do good works, which are the fruit of our salvation. It is God's work for and in man. We cooperate and submit to the Lord, united with Him. Our old man is gone and our new man is born. We obey, not because we need to earn anything, but out of the overflow of joy and love we find as we obey, which brings us and God delight. In obedience we become more like Him and have fullness of heart for God and for others. Our obedience is a continual process of sanctification.

As He works in us, He begins sanctifying us. Paul expressed this process. After conversion we continue to grow. He said, "I do not understand what I do. For what I want to do I do not do, but what I hate I do" (Romans 7:15, NIV). We need grace before and after salvation. We are works in progress who are becoming more and more conformed to Christ's likeness as we walk with Jesus in relationship. Grace is available to us once we know Christ. We are being perfected, but until we see Him face to face in His Kingdom, we require great grace and mercy.

Just as a trained paramedic administers CPR to a lifeless body and gets the heart pumping again, Christ gives us CPR— Christ Purchased Redemption. We enter into His restoration: Operation Resurrection. I was dead, and Christ made me alive by His resurrection power. Having His Spirit alive and powerful in us transforms us from the inside out. He is in us to direct and change and empower us by His grace.

THE TAX COLLECTOR AND THE PHARISEE

Today, if I saw that young man, I know what I would tell him, because it is a message my own ears needed to hear for so long. I would say, "I'm so sorry that you received such a letter. But let's see what Jesus said." I would then take him to the Bible passage about the tax collector and the Pharisee.

He also told this parable to some people who trusted in themselves *and* were confident that they were righteous [posing outwardly as upright and in right standing with God], and who viewed others with contempt: "Two men went up into the temple [enclosure] to pray, one a Pharisee and the other a tax collector. The Pharisee stood [ostentatiously] and began praying to himself [in a self-righteous way, saying]: 'God, I thank You that I am not like the rest of men—swindlers, unjust (dishonest), adulterers—or even like this tax collector. I fast twice a week; I pay tithes of all that I get.' But the tax collector, standing at a distance, would not even raise his eyes toward heaven, but was striking his chest [in humility and repentance], saying, 'God, be merciful *and* gracious to me, the [especially wicked] sinner [that I am]!' I tell you, this man went to his home justified [forgiven of the guilt of sin and placed in right standing with God] rather than the other man; for everyone who exalts himself will be humbled, but he who humbles himself [forsaking self-righteous pride] will be exalted" (Luke 18:9-14, AMP).

After reading the verses, I would ask the young man to put himself in the story and to put his aunt within the passage, too. I would explain that God hates self-righteousness and pride and is not in agreement with those that think that they are good enough in their own good works. These people miss what Christ came to do—save the lost. God is merciful to those that repent! I would share the fact of Christ's death to forgive his sins and give him a new heart and life, and together, God willing, we would pray, asking God to help him repent and receive the gifts of grace from Christ. Why did it take me so long to understand this?

If we confess our sins, he is faithful and just to forgive us our sins,
and to cleanse us from all unrighteousness. 1 John 1:9, KJV

And rend your heart, and not your garments, and turn unto the Lord your God:
for he is gracious and merciful, slow to anger, and of great kindness,… Joel 2:13, KJV

To the Lord our God belong mercies and forgivenesses,
though we have rebelled against him. Daniel 9:9, KJV

THE GOSPEL TRUTH

Each of us—the aunt, the young man, me and you—must see our own need, depravity, and inability to be good enough, so we can receive what Christ has done for us on the cross. He was judged on our behalf. When we receive Christ as our Savior, we receive His payment for our judgement. We are fully forgiven and redeemed, and we have hope! It is good news!

The true Gospel reveals God's acceptance of the judgment of sin by Jesus so we could be declared not guilty. Christ paid the penalty by His sacrificial death. Therefore, it is important to understand:

- that morality alone is not what pleases God;
- that if we could be good and moral, we would not need a Savior;
- that Satan's version of good is a counterfeit;
- that grace changes people;
- that grace was paid in full by Christ's blood; and
- that living in the new identity of Christ through being born again changes our nature.

NEAR TO THE BROKENHEARTED

The young man at the lockdown facility appeared hopeless, yet his heart seemed to yearn to be accepted just as he was. I heard in his voice recognition that he had fallen short, and he needed someone or something to save him.

In the years since that encounter, I've discovered verses that may have helped that teenager.

The Lord is near to the brokenhearted. And saves those who are crushed in spirit (Psalm 34:18, NASB).

Jesus loves the brokenhearted and discouraged. He offers mercy, hope, and healing and He is near. And we need not work to receive these gifts from Him. We need only come to Christ for the gift of God: forgiveness, acceptance into His family, and eternal life.

What I needed to experience at a deeper level—and what that teenager needed to receive—was the saved-by-grace-alone-through-Christ-alone Gospel. Jesus Christ took our sin, its curse, and its consequences of death and hell. That's the "He-died-in-our-place-while-we-were-yet-sinners" Gospel. (See Romans 5:8.)

Now that—that is the Gospel of hope.

LIVING MEMORIALS

Erwin Lutzer once said in a radio broadcast that we should not be offended at what God allows. Instead we should look for His purposes, plans, and redemption. God has been very good to me. Yet life has been so very hard. Can you relate? Joni Erickson Tada said, "God permits what He hates, to accomplish what He loves." She also said, "Splash-overs of heaven are when you find Jesus in the splash-over of hell." Both of these statements encouraged me as I think of the amazing truth and amazing grace of Jesus.

These words are soothing to me because I believe He has a plan for my life.

Because the Lord works all things together for good for us who love Him (Romans 8:28), we have assurance that whatever we have done or whatever we were victims of can be used to bring about good. The terrible events of my first 21 years of life are turning into good pictures of God's redemption. Because I am so convinced of God's Work on my behalf—His purchasing my redemption—I am able to share my story. God exchanges the bad for the wonderful and amazing through Jesus. Where else can you take your rags and receive riches? Your lies are exchanged for His truth at His cross.

The scars or wounds and torment of old sins and their shame are turned to memorials of God's grace for "where sin increased, grace abounded all the more," (Romans 5:20). Let the whole earth stand in amazement and awe of Him and His grace. He is our God and did all we needed to be right with Him and live as the people of His portion. We are to be confident of the redeeming work of God. The wrath of God was satisfied for every sin was laid on Christ. The God of Israel has visited and redeemed us. We have been bought with the precious blood of Jesus. The price was high. It was paid and was enough to cover all our sins and to take them away.

WHAT SATAN MEANT FOR EVIL

My paraphrase of Genesis 50:20 is "what Satan meant for harm, God will use for good." God's ways are higher than our ways. In the midst of my despair, Christ was and is there for me—my only complete help. He is the only one who fully understands, loves, and accepts me. I am believing God to make my life, my mess, our mess, our marriage beautiful. It has taken the supernatural intervention of God for us to live the Gospel to ourselves and each other. Through Christ, we have received forgiveness; loved and forgiven ourselves and each other.

Please do not believe the lie that the Christian life will not work for you as it does for others, or that you are too bad to be redeemed. This is a spiritual attack of lies that often brings mental breakdown, anxiety, feelings of worthlessness, fear, and anxiety. We can work all our lives to improve ourselves and our self-perception, but nothing works eternally, effectively, or everyday like Christ's life in us. To have Christ is to have life. We must understand how to fight the spiritual demonic warfare and its effect on our minds. Submit to God, resist the devil and he will flee. (James 4:7) God loves you and wants your redemption. Christ paid for your redemption with His own blood. We need to recite the Gospel to ourselves daily.

Being aware and savoring the happiness of Christ as the indescribable gift is what the Lord wants. His love came down for us, for this purpose. To God, we were worth His death. Because He is love, for the joy set before Him, He endured the cross, and in His love at the cross we are in truth and He brings His favor and grace. He is our hope. (Hebrews 12:2; 1 Peter 1.)

YOUR VALUABLE SOUL

Why does God care about changing our lives and saving the worst kind of person? Because He values us. Billy Graham put it this way.

> *"Jesus said that your soul is worth more than the rest of the world put together. Why is your soul so valuable? First, the value of your soul is measured by its eternal quality. It will never die. ...Your soul—your spirit—will live forever. Second, the value of your soul is measured by the devil's interest in it. Jesus said the devil is the prince of this world. He is the god of this age. The devil is greatly at work in our world, and he is after your soul. Third, the value of your soul is measured by God's concern for saving your soul. Fourth, the value of your soul is measured by the severity of its loss. Fifth, the value of your soul is measured by the price paid for its redemption (the precious blood of Christ, as of a lamb without blemish and without spot 1 Peter 1:18-19)."*[8]

Our only hope is God. Not limited hope—great hope, because God is infinite and He is love (see Ephesians 3:8a). His blood purchased our souls at the cost of His death. Without God we have no hope, but with God all hope is unleashed, because we gain the incalculable riches of Christ (see Ephesians 3:8b). Let us not discount the power of God for salvation for any who will believe. Our souls are valuable, and Christ paid the most valuable price—His life.

HOPE, NOT "HOPE SO"

Paul said this of his own story,

"Christ Jesus came into the world to save sinners—of whom I am the worst. But for that very reason I was shown mercy so that in me, the worst of sinners, Christ Jesus might display his immense patience as an example for those who would believe in him and receive eternal life." (1 Timothy 1:15-16, NIV)

The most unlikeable, antagonistic people can be transformed into the greatest proponents of the Gospel, because they have experienced the power of God. When God transforms you personally, you know transformation is possible for others. Paul was a murderer, transformed into a champion for the Gospel. I want to be a champion too, by heralding the champion's cause—the Gospel. Christ gave Paul hope. Not a hope so hope, but hope Himself. Christ is hope. He gave Paul Himself! (1 Timothy 1:1; Colossians 1:27) In Christ we have peace. (John 16:33)

When we are in Christ, we are a new creation, the old is gone and the new has come. And if we confess our sins, He is faithful and just to forgive our sins.

The Life of the Secret of Hope

A life lived according to the secret of hope is a life that follows the Gospel cycle. It is losing yourself and gaining Christ, depending on Him as your first love and source of power. It is living covenant love, willingness to give when not getting back; willingness to lay down our lives for another even when being rejected.

It is costly and sacrificial love. It is a losing of our life to gain identification with the life of Christ. Christ's heart bore our sins and was broken and bled for us. His hope was deferred. He was rejected so we could be accepted. The secret of our hope is in this fact. He restored our hope through His hopelessness. Our hope lives because of His resurrection!

We are to follow His lead. Our own hearts have been broken by others' sins against us. So we relate to love's betrayals and the cost of love's unconditional covenant. Christ knows where our hearts have been sick. He wants us to learn how to live victoriously in His secret of hope. Because of Him, we can preach hope to our souls in the places where hopelessness tries to flourish. Loving God more is my greatest life goal and comes from His love for me and its hope!

I am still learning how to live and explain the mystery of Christ's hope. It is infinite and it is dynamic, active, lively and so very hard to comprehend in my finite understanding. I do know, though, that living hope is promised in Christ! (1Peter1:3-5; 1 Tim 1:1, Colossians 1:27)

Writing this book and processing my past has strengthened my desire to more fully live in and herald the fullness of our great salvation. It is the secret to true hope. I can say as the Samaritan woman said, "Come, see a man who told me all that I ever did. Can this be the Christ?" He is the Christ; He proved it to me.

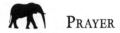 ## Prayer

Dear LORD, help us recognize that because of what your incomparable love accomplished at the cross, we have hope offered to us. Our only hope is in you, trading our powerlessness for your power. Help us guard against the enemy, Satan, who wants us to miss what you came to give. Please protect us from discouragement, condemnation, and the judgments of others. Embolden us, despite opposition, to live and speak the true Gospel of God (1 Thessalonians 2:2). In Christ's saving name, amen.

4

THE HOPE OF FORGIVENESS

Blessed is the one whose transgression is forgiven, whose sin is covered. (Psalm 32:1, NIV)

"Oh what we could be if we stopped carrying the remains of who we were." -Tyler Knott Gregson

God's Holy Spirit's great grace poured out through Peter to the group of people that crucified Christ and offered them salvation. Three thousand were saved. (Acts 2-4, summary)

If you, O LORD, kept a record of sins, O LORD, who could stand? But with you there is forgiveness, therefore, you are feared. (Psalm 130:3-4, NIV)

The voice of sin is loud, but the voice of forgiveness is louder.[9] ~Dwight L. Moody

After many years, I told my dear Catholic father of our abortion, hoping to share my heart and my experience of the Gospel with him and perhaps to find acceptance despite our failure.

But Dad told me God could not forgive me for my sin. At that moment the Holy Spirit rose in me and I boldly declared, "You are so right, Dad, if I was depending on my being forgiven by what I can do, but I am depending on Christ's forgiveness based on what He did!"

No wonder I had tried so hard to be good. I wanted to be forgiven. When I needed hope I felt hopeless. When I wanted someone to give me the hope of forgiveness, I was met with words and told to do works that did not work. Dead end to the dead line.

I can't blame others for my pain, because I couldn't seem to forgive myself either. My religion was works-based; it was and still tries to be a burden and a hindrance. I believed the only pathway to relief from my pain was to do something good. I did not understand that forgiveness was freely available because of Jesus and the cross.

THE KEY TO HOPE

Before I understood forgiveness based on the work of Christ, I couldn't tell my story.

How could I still think I had to earn forgiveness—as if there was some giant scale that I could balance out my sin by doing good? Sadly, my religion hindered me (as it was my foundational training, my circus-elephant shackling), until Christ revealed to me the freedom He had earned for me. I am forgiven because of Jesus. As I have more fully accepted Jesus' forgiveness, I have begun living the true Gospel, forgiving myself by acknowledging the greatness of forgiveness earned and granted to me through Christ.

My early training was hard to completely overcome. The door to the prison of my mind was open but somehow my trained thinking, my circumstances, and other people kept shackling me and taking me back inside the prison, despite the open door and invitation of freedom to go outside it! The lies kept being reinforced. I needed more truth.

There was hope for me somewhere. What I didn't know was that Christ and His forgiveness was the key.

So many times I thought, *I am beyond forgiveness. I can never recover.* I am not alone. There are many who believe these lies. Religion of works reinforced these lies. Christ's life, work, truth, Gospel proves otherwise. Forgiveness is a gift that Christ died for me to gain.

FORGIVEN COMPLETELY

Nothing could be better than to be forgiven completely and treated as if you are innocent—even though you are guilty of murder, or perhaps of something worse. To experience love's rescue at the cost of the death of your rescuer is the essence of the Gospel, God's amazing love. Christ's murder on the cross reversed death's hold, brought life, and opened the way to heaven for any who will believe. Jesus Christ is Lord, and God raised Him from the dead. When you believe in Christ, God raises you—from spiritual death to life both eternal and secure. What can be better than that? The offer for full redemption, full acceptance, and full eternal love is given unconditionally to anybody— whosoever will believe.

One verse that helped me is from Paul's letter to the Ephesians. "And be ye kind one to another, tenderhearted, forgiving one another, even as God for Christ's sake hath forgiven you" (Ephesians 4:32, KJV). Notice the phrase that explains why God has forgiven—"for Christ's sake." Because of Christ and all that He accomplished, I am forgiven by God. This truth is Gospel. To not forgive is to say that what Christ did is not enough to redeem it. To forgive is to agree Christ's death is enough.

Today we have the surpassing grace of God and His incomparable forgiveness offered and yet so many refuse. The Son of God died at the hands of mankind and then mankind denies His death and its significance. In so doing, they cancel their grace card—their get-out-of-hell-free card. It costs God His Son and they say, "no thanks."

CHOOSING TO REJECT

We aren't the first to deal with hard questions. Billy Graham was asked if God will forgive murder. He wrote the answer in his column.

> Question:
> Dear Dr. Graham: I've been in jail for almost 20 years for killing a man during an armed robbery. The chaplain here says God will forgive me, but I can't make myself believe it. I know I don't deserve any mercy, either from the courts or from God. Isn't killing someone the unforgivable sin? -- W.W.

> Answer:
> Dear W.W.: Murder is a terrible crime -- but no, it isn't the unforgivable sin. The only sin God cannot forgive is the sin of turning our backs on Him and refusing to accept His forgiveness.

After He has shown His friendship, loyalty, and unconditional love—sacrifice at the greatest cost—it is unimaginable to shun His gift, resist Him, reject and betray His goodness. To do so carries its own result of death forever—permanent eternal separation from God.

WORSE THAN MURDER

Let's consider a question. Is there anything worse than crucifying Christ? The answer is yes, because to miss, reject, or not receive the gifts His death accomplished is to make His death "be in vain." As if someone rescued you while you were dead in the water already having drowned—he or she goes in after you, gets you to shore, does CPR and uses his or her very last breath to bring you life and in so doing the rescuer dies. But you then commit suicide and curse the one who died to save you. It is not a perfect illustration. However, it shows the denial and cost of the rescue. Matthew 23:37 and 1 Thessalonians 2:14-16 convey this concept in Scripture.

"O Jerusalem, Jerusalem, thou that killest the prophets, and stonest them which are sent unto thee, how often would I have gathered thy children together, even as a hen gathereth her chickens under her wings, and ye would not" (Matthew 23:37, KJV).

Christ wept over Jerusalem. He knew the hearts of the people He came to save. He knew they were murderers; they had killed the prophets of God…yet He longed to bring them under His saving wing like a mother her babes—but they would not come. Their rejection broke Jesus' heart. Knowing He would die a terrible death and pour out all He had for them, yet they would not receive His gifts or receive Him.

Consider the Judas trail of betrayal. Judas experienced the divinity of Christ, the magnitude of His majesty, and the essence of God over and over during the years he traveled with the Lord. He was shown the presence of the eternal, omnipotent King of kings, creator, sustainer, life-giving God. The fullness of the Godhead, the image of the invincible God, the exact representation of God's being, the radiance of His glory, yet Judas chose to reject and betray.

Someone may say, I wasn't alive at the time Jesus Christ was on earth, so why should I care about Jesus? The answer is hope—it is only through acceptance of His life, death, and resurrection that whatever you have done in life can be erased in God's economy and you can be forgiven and received as though you have never sinned. Salvation is great news. And it means that you are forgiven even if you had an abortion or have been deep in sexual sin or have been a thief or a liar or extortionist or drug addict or alcoholic or a hellion…. Everything and anything can be forgiven by Jesus when repentance truly happens.

You can be made truly new—no longer the person you used to be. He doesn't wait for us to clean up ourselves; He took our place in death so we could live abundantly and would have a way to heaven. For further evidence of God's great grace, you may want to read Acts chapters 1-4 to see how Peter preached to the group of people that crucified Christ and offered them salvation. Three thousand were saved. Christ wants to forgive anyone and everyone, and does not want any to perish!

Even given the amazing grace of God we see the resistance of those that refuse His truth and love persist. See 1 Thessalonians 2:14-16

I IDENTIFY

As I have struggled for courage, fortitude, and motivation to go forward, I have found significant help in the Scriptures—in the lives of Peter, Paul, and the woman at the well.

Jesus dealt kindly, mercifully, and graciously with each of these. He forgave them much, and I knew He had forgiven me much.

I identify with Paul in my early life in following the rules and doing the right thing. I thought I was good and righteous in my works and thinking, and I thought that I pleased God and was right with God. But, like Paul, I did not have a saving relationship with Him at all.

I identify with Peter because too often I depend on my own abilities and try to prove myself and my loyalty. I have been prideful, self-righteous, and have denied Christ by hiding my past and what Christ has done for me.

I identify with the Samaritan woman because after I endured occult abuse, I became so much of what I hated and much of what I knew God hated. I lived in sexual debauchery for a season. I broke the commandments. I felt my sins and I had great shame. I was an outcast and felt defiled—worthless.

I turned back to Jesus in full repentance yet I knew that if people in the church knew my story, I would fare no better than that Samaritan woman. The disciples did not want to talk to her or identify with her. Over the centuries, some things do not easily change.

In identifying with these three real people, I have prayed regularly to be "converted more completely," to be turned to God and not to live for myself. I believe the Lord has taken me to hopeless places to teach me that in hopelessness and powerlessness, He offers me Christ and He brings forgiveness, strength, conversion, and transformation.

HOPE FOR HEALING

Reading a blog about hope and healing for those who have had an abortion, I noticed that the teen author expressed sorrow for allowing her boyfriend to convince her to abort their baby. She seemed to want closure, peace, and assurance. She warned readers, "Do not tell me that I killed my baby and will go to hell." She wrote that she was not open to "Bible bashers," and said she was well aware of what the Bible said.

The most glaring omission in her blog was what is actually in the Bible about forgiveness and grace and mercy.

Christ forgives sins—even abortion. God delights in mercy. Mercy can triumph. The numbers of men and women who are post-abortive are staggering in the United States alone. Statistically, it has been said that regret and guilt from abortion is the most common experience of our generation.[10]

Christ's cross is about love and forgiveness, not condemnation. It is heartbreaking that so many people who have personally experienced abortion don't receive a full explanation of mercy and forgiveness. They are kept at a distance, judged, and even ostracized by some in the church. Further, that so many have been taught to think that God is against them, and shackled to belief that there is no remedy for the guilt, even though full remedy and full forgiveness is available at the cross of Jesus by His love!

FORGIVENESS FOR MURDER

On another occasion, Billy Graham wrote about forgiveness.

> *Question:*
> *I'm in prison because I got angry and killed someone, and I'm haunted by guilt. Someone told me that Jesus forgave a murderer once, but when I challenged him to prove it he couldn't find it in the Bible. I wish I could believe God will forgive me, but I can't.*
>
> *Answer:*
> *"What you did was serious; in fact, almost nothing is more serious in the eyes of God (and of society) than deliberately taking an innocent person's life. The Ten Commandments state it clearly: "You shall not murder" (Exodus 20:13).*
>
> *But there is only one sin that God cannot forgive — and that is the sin of refusing His forgiveness. Yes, you committed a great sin — but you would be committing an even greater sin if you rejected God's forgiveness. And that is what He offers you! You may hate what you've done; you may even hate yourself for doing it. But God still loves you, and He yearns for you to come to Him and be with Him in Heaven through all eternity.*
>
> *How do I know this? One reason is because your acquaintance was right: Jesus Christ even forgave a murderer. Who was it? It was Saul of Tarsus — who became the Apostle Paul, the greatest Christian who ever lived! At one time Saul hated Christians, and was responsible for sending many of them to their death: "I persecuted the followers of this Way to their death" (Acts 22:4).*
>
> *But God forgave him and changed his life — and the same can happen to you. Don't carry your burden of guilt any longer, but by faith turn to Jesus Christ and give it to Him. Then ask Him to come into your life and cleanse you of all your sins — and He will."[11]*

God forgave Moses, David, and Paul who had all murdered. Moses slew an Egyptian taskmaster in anger when he saw him beating an Israelite slave, but through God's divine purpose, Moses became the leader of the entire Israelite people on their Exodus from Egypt. David arranged for a man to be killed because he did not want his adultery to be discovered, but God forgave him when he truly repented and sought forgiveness (see Psalm 32; Psalm 51). Saul was responsible for putting Christians in prison and arranging for their executions -- but God forgave him, and Saul of Tarsus became the Apostle Paul, who touched the Roman Empire with the Gospel and wrote much of the New Testament.

God forgave each one and then worked mighty miracles in their lives. Though we may think murder is unforgivable, God's love and forgiveness is greater than any sin. Jesus forgave those who crucified Him. His Gospel includes forgiveness of murder. Yes, God can forgive a murderer, because He already has.

GOD WANTS TO FORGIVE US

But I also know God can forgive even a murderer because He *wants* to forgive us! You see, you and I were responsible for Jesus' death, because our sins caused Him to die. If you and I had not sinned, Jesus wouldn't have had to go to the cross—but we are sinners, and He died for us.

Why did He do that? He did it because God loves us, and He wants to forgive us so we can spend eternity with Him in heaven. Don't delay any longer, but give your life to Christ and accept His gift of forgiveness today. The Bible says, "Seek the Lord while he may be found. ... for he will abundantly pardon" (Isaiah 55:6-7, NASB).

A FURTHER TRUTH OF FORGIVENESS

Jesus tells me if I do not forgive, I cannot be forgiven. "And forgive us our debts, as we also have forgiven our debtors." Matthew 6:12. Since my forgiveness is solely based on Christ, to not extend the same grace I have been given is to be an unmerciful servant (Matthew 18). I must forgive. Not only must I forgive others, but I must be forgiving toward myself.

We victims do not ever have to be okay with what happened to us. It is not okay what others have done, but we can be okay. We can turn to God in our pain. We can forgive through the access we have to God's power through Christ. By choosing forgiveness we eventually become okay in our spirits and our souls. We can choose to love like we have never been hurt and forgive. That is the Jesus way. It helps me when I remember that nobody has ever done more to show me that I am *unloved* than Christ has done on the cross to show me I am *loved*.[12] His example to us gives us no room to remain in unforgiveness. Love and forgiveness is what we are to live and then trust God for all the rest. To forgive is to give the judgment to God, for Him to deal with the person His way. It takes God to accomplish full forgiveness in us but we must be willing. It is a part of the secret of hope: where I am unable, Jesus is able.

Sometimes forgiving yourself and forgiving those closest to us is the hardest journey that continues daily until glory. When I began to really forgive as a lifestyle (not just an intellectual theology, but a living reality of my theology), the forgiveness began to show in practical daily life and through an increase of trust and respect for my husband. Forgiving myself and accepting myself also increased. A belief in the "us" I once knew began to be reborn. It's been a process. A process toward victory.

THE VICTORY OF THE CROSS

I am convinced one of the greatest strategies of Satan is to try to convince us that the Gospel does not work—to send us back into trying to keep the Law. He attempts to diminish the cross and the forgiveness of sins based on Christ's work, because Satan knows the arsenal of God's power for man is at the cross. The greatest place of victory is the cross. The greatest reversals are possible there. Satan accuses, condemns, and perverts grace, bringing unbelief, stealing our faith, and attempting to weaken our understanding of the cross and its power and victory. He wants us to miss what Christ came to gain. Our only hope is in Christ and His grace. For we have overcome by the blood of the Lamb and the word of our testimony and we are to live our lives to prove its truth. (Revelation 12:11).

PAUL WAS FORGIVEN

Paul explained this free, yet costly, grace in another verse from his letter. "To me, [though I am] the very least of all the saints (God's people), this grace [which is undeserved] was graciously given, to proclaim to the Gentiles the good news of the incomprehensible riches of Christ [that spiritual wealth which no one can fully understand"] (Ephesians 3:8, AMP).

Paul was an unlikely candidate to be an ambassador for Christ. In his early years, he studied under the most intellectual and respected rabbi of the day. He became an expert in the law and Jewish traditions and was elevated to the position of a chief Pharisee. He participated in the persecution of the people who followed Christ and ultimately became one of the chief persecutors with threats and imprisonment. But one day, Jesus appeared to Paul and commissioned him.

> Get up and stand on your feet. I have appeared to you for this purpose, to
> appoint you [to serve] as a minister and as a witness [to testify, with authority,]

not only to the things which you have seen, but also to the things in which I will appear to you, [choosing you for Myself and] rescuing you from the *Jewish* people and from the Gentiles, to whom I am sending you, to open their [spiritual] eyes so that they may turn from darkness to light and from the power of Satan to God, that they may receive forgiveness *and* release from their sins and an inheritance among those who have been sanctified (set apart, made holy) by faith in me (Acts 26:16-18, AMP).

Imagine. Jesus saved—and then called, appointed, and anointed—a persecutor, a murderer of those who followed Him. In his old life, Paul thought he was doing the right thing, but wasn't. He missed Jesus until Jesus opened his eyes by revelation. From that moment forward, Paul's life shows repentance, trust, and devotion to Christ. Jesus assigned Paul the mission of telling people that they may receive forgiveness and be released from their sins. Paul, who had terribly persecuted believers in his past, heralded Christ's message and became one of God's greatest witnesses.

The Lord had a job for Paul, and He has a job for us to do, too. *No matter our past.* If we repent of our sin and put our faith in Christ for forgiveness, we are redeemed. Christ indwells us. He has handpicked us to be a servant and witness for the power of God to salvation.

Our mission is to go and tell all the world what God has done for us, preach the Gospel, and make disciples.

CHRIST THE FORGIVER

I most want others to know through this brief writing what has taken great suffering, great sorrow, and great agony for me to learn through decades-long journey. I no longer want to live a foolish version of the Gospel. Living religiously fails miserably. Letting religious people define you could kill you. Waiting for others to affirm you is a setup for disappointing heartsickness.

Living for Christ works, yet it does not always feel like it works. We must believe the truth despite our feelings. Be prepared, because the enemy hits us with doubt, and he is relentless in trying to convince us that we have no hope, even though we have been forgiven. People who have had abortions are forgiven because of Christ's blood. Forgiveness gives us a clean conscience and life. Anyone who has been sexually abused, occult abused, or religiously abused can be healed and live in peace and victory. Even when it doesn't feel true, it's true.

Forgiving our abusers and anyone involved in our pain helps us forgive ourselves. As we forgive others and ourselves, we begin to feel the forgiveness of Christ. But even if we don't feel forgiven, we can know we are forgiven. Feelings can be deceiving. We must base our truth on fact, not on feelings. Feelings can eventually line up with the truth. It takes time.

On Twitter on July 16, 2016, Ravi Zacharias posted this: "None of the problems outside will be solved until the problem inside is solved."

But the war within can end. The conflict and shame, the accusation, the exploitation, the worthlessness, and the utter hopelessness can be resolved. No sin is too great for our great Savior, Christ Jesus. He sees all we have ever done, knows everything we have ever thought, and hears every word we have ever spoken—yet He loves us unconditionally. Jesus died to take away our sin. He takes it all away. We do not have to live with the shame or guilt anymore.

That is why I can write these things—because He has taken my sins away. Forgiveness does not mean that there are no consequences; yet even in them, there is hope. Forgiveness is the hard work of the Gospel and it takes faith in Christ to live it to the fullest of what it really is eternally. God has promised redemption and Romans 8:28 is an assurance and comfort. There is hope in His many promises. Hope in the inheritance, which He promises. Knowing Christ is eternal and abundant life. (Psalm 16; John 10.)

The Anointing that Breaks the Yoke

Eventually, my dad expressed a greater experience of the forgiveness of Christ. He shared with me how he had experienced God's love in a more personal way than in his younger years, and said that he wished he had understood earlier in life what he now knew. He said it is such a better life knowing Jesus than just knowing about Him. Dad reassured me he was going to heaven based on the work of Jesus on the cross for the forgiveness of his sins.

I thank God for the anointing that breaks and broke the yoke. (Isaiah 10:27, KJV) The oppression of man's work, the oppression of this world and the enemy is broken by the work of God by His Anointed Son Christ Jesus! Jesus said, "Father, forgive them, for they do not know what they are doing." (Luke 23:34.) Forgiveness has been accomplished. Christ's way is the only way of eternal forgiveness. It cost Christ His life for me to have full eternal forgiveness. I gladly give Christ my life to share the greatness of His forgiveness for the debt of the guilt and shame of sins being paid and His gifts of hope and inheritance.

Conclusion

I questioned God how to determine when to lay down in submission to His will and plan and when to stand up to unrighteousness with truth, grace and love. I had submitted to abortion in my marriage that first year and that was not what I should have done. Now I would not submit to denying the real truth but instead fight for the truth and apply forgiveness to myself and others and herald the Gospel.

The burden of unforgiveness was great. It was like carrying double my weight and my husband's around on my back, like a backpack with straps extending around my neck that had been choking the life out of me! It was a prison of weight. Living forgiveness has granted release and the entrapment of being an unmerciful unforgiving one is finally gone! (Matthew 9:12; Matthew 18:21-35.) Christ has forgiven me (Luke 23:34). Gospel living is leaving the burden of our old selves, all our sins, our shame, our offenses, and unforgiveness of ourselves and others at the cross. We have stopped "carrying the remains of who we were"! We are moving forward as new creations. We have the love and forgiveness In Christ!

As I follow Christ's example of forgiving those who have wounded me, God promises to work things out for good. (Genesis 50:20, Romans 8:28). My early victimization was unjust and undeserved and set me up for so much of my suffering and sin. I am forgiven for my sins. Now, I am encouraged that the Lord will use my sufferings and wounds and my living forgiveness to lead others to Christ for healing too. His way of healing us was completed at His death on the cross and His resurrection. The God of Hope became hopeless (suffered, died, was buried) for us to have hope. In my sufferings in my places of greatest hopelessness I now see God bringing forth hope for me, our family and others. My husband's favorite Psalm is Psalm 103. Here are some of the reminders of the greatness of God's forgiveness and grace:

1 Praise the Lord, my soul; all my inmost being, praise his holy name.
2 Praise the Lord, my soul,and forget not all his benefits—
3 who forgives all your sins and heals all your diseases,
4 who redeems your life from the pit
8 The Lord is compassionate and gracious, slow to anger, abounding in love
10 he does not treat us as our sins deserve or repay us according to our iniquities.
11 For as high as the heavens are above the earth,so great is his love for those who fear him;
12 as far as the east is from the west, so far has he removed our transgressions from us.
13 As a father has compassion on his children,so the Lord has compassion on those who fear him;
(Psalm 103:1-4, 8, 10-13, NIV)

 PRAYER

LORD God, compassionate and gracious, slow to anger, and abounding in lovingkindness and truth; who is a God like you, who pardons sin and forgives the transgression of His people? You do not stay angry forever but delight to show mercy (Micah 7:18). You have compassion on us, no matter what we have done! Please call to your people to come take shelter under your cover of forgiveness at the cross. LORD, we thank you that if we confess our sins, you are faithful and just to forgive us our sins and to cleanse us from all unrighteousness (1 John 1:9). Help us to live in the fullness of what you purchased for us by accepting the forgiveness that cost you your life (Luke 23:34) and extending that forgiveness to others. In Christ's saving name, amen.

HOPE FOR YOUR STORY

Then he turned my sorrow into joy! He took away my clothes of mourning and clothed me with joy so that I might sing glad praises to the Lord instead of lying in silence in the grave. O Lord my God, I will keep on thanking you forever! (Psalm 30:11-12, TLB)

Let the redeemed of the LORD tell their story-- those he redeemed from the hand of the foe. (Psalm 107:2, NIV.)

*Regardless of how put together they look, many ...have broken stories....
God is the healer of emotional, relational, and sexual brokenness....
He has the power to redeem your pain and story too.*[13]

"How our lives bear the fruit of Christ's spilled blood is important. The stories of our lives can serve to encourage and warn others. But telling the stories of our lives is heady business."[14] *Rosaria Butterfield*

As I recovered at home after surgery to correct a serious spinal injury a faithful pastor friend, whom I love like a brother, brought me a book titled *The Secret Thoughts of an Unlikely Convert.* That book opened up a whole new world of authentically following Christ.

As I read the honest assessment of Christianity and about the vulnerable position of the author, Rosaria Butterfield, I was stunned. She was forthright, even blunt, when telling her life story. Her first words, "When I was 28 years old, I boldly declared myself lesbian," hit me like a train wreck. She had done what she could to advance radical leftist ideologies (pro-choice and pro-gay lifestyles), and she genuinely believed that she was helping to make the world a better place. Then she said that at 36 years of age, "Christ claimed me for himself, and the life that I had known and loved came to a humiliating end."

She was more honest, forthright and courageous than I had been in more than 40 years as a believer. The enormity of my hypocrisy was searing and I burned with conviction. I had been living as a hypocrite, and she was living as Paul modeled.

I came face to face with the worst sins of my life. I was being called to come clean and tell of what great things Christ has done for me and share the Gospel with the world, to show my "leprosy" so that I could also demonstrate His healing.

I believe all Christians are called to have this experience! Paul did. Peter did. Anyone who hopes to have a great impact on the world will also. Because Christ died that others might be saved, we need to promote Christ and His saving grace. We are first to experience the greatness of our salvation so we will want to give out His great salvation message to the world.

I mentioned it before, and I will say it again here: God's desire is that all our stories be redeemed. Getting there involves a series of choices. First the acceptance of Christ's life for your salvation—and then the processing and acceptance of the forgiveness of God, that it's really for you, personally, and that you can in fact forgive those who have hurt you. In this chapter, I want to start a discussion about the boldness that springs from redemption and leads to announcing and heralding the truth of Christ's life in your life.

Owning Your Story

If you owed a trillion-dollar debt you could never repay it. What if someone paid your debt in full, but the repayment caused that someone to die? You are rescued and redeemed, but they died. Would you tell the story? Of course, especially if it had the surprise and amazing ending where the person was supernaturally resurrected. That story is the story of Christ. You are surrounded by debtors and you have the key to the debt reversal agent. We herald the Gospel by telling our stories because He has rescued us, is ready to rescue others, and He is alive.

Regarding sharing my story, many friends have told me, "Don't do it!" or given the impression of "If you do, don't expect us to do it, too!" Some have said, "I could never be so open to let my children and others know what I have done."

My husband and I talked about this. He said, "The Lord knows, and what matters is that we took our sin to Him and repented. By His grace and mercy, He has forgiven us. Confession to anybody else is a very distant second place." Yet, we have come to realize that confessing our sins to others is the way to healing (James 5:16). It was not until we began doing this in earnest that the completion of our healing has come about, especially in our relationship.

We agree that giving testimony could help others know that they too can be fully forgiven, as we show them Gospel living through living out Revelation 12:11, Psalm 103, Psalm 51, and the rest of the Bible!

CONFESSION: GOOD FOR THE SOUL

Confessing our sins, first to Christ and sometimes also to one to another (prayerfully, when led by the Holy Spirit), is a vital part of the Christian life. James 5:16, Scripture says, "Therefore, confess your sins to one another and pray for each other so that you may be healed."

In 1 John 1:8-10 (NLT) we read: 8 If we claim we have no sin, we are only fooling ourselves and not living in the truth. 9 But if we confess our sins to him, he is faithful and just to forgive us our sins and to cleanse us from all wickedness. 10 If we claim we have not sinned, we are calling God a liar and showing that his word has no place in our hearts.

We find healing and cleansing in the act of opening those dark corners of our stories. We let the light in, and it illuminates us and floods us with healing power. Confession is powerful.

Max Lucado says:

> Confession isn't telling God what he doesn't know. That's impossible. It's not pointing fingers at others without pointing any at me. That may feel good, but it doesn't promote healing. Confession is a radical reliance on grace—a trust in God's goodness. The truth is, confessors find a freedom that deniers don't! Tell God what you did. Again, it's not that he doesn't already know, but the two of you need to agree! Then let the pure water of grace flow over your mistakes! [15]

THE HIDDEN HEART OF HOPE

There is an added dimension to our testimony. We not only tell the Gospel, but we are also to show or live the Gospel. Christ in us, the hope of glory (Colossians 1:27) helps us conquer the enemy in the telling and the living of the Gospel. We have a new heart, a hidden hope, that we are to make known. We want our lives to show the power of the Gospel to conquer sin. Paul's life is proof. Our lives are to be also. All who know Christ are to be conformed to His image. Our lives are to give testimony of God's overcoming.

> And they have conquered him by the blood of the Lamb and by the word of their testimony, for they loved not their lives even unto death (Revelation 12:11, ESV).

> My mouth will tell of your righteous acts, of your deeds of salvation all the day, for their number is past my knowledge. With the mighty deeds of the

Lord God I will come; I will remind them of your righteousness, yours alone. (Psalm 71:15-16, ESV)

So everyone who acknowledges me before men, I also will acknowledge before my Father who is in heaven (Matthew 10:32, ESV).

But in your hearts honor Christ the Lord as holy, always being prepared to make a defense to anyone who asks you for a reason for the hope that is in you; yet do it with gentleness and respect (1 Peter 3:15, ESV).

Sharing our story is a matter of obedience.

It is hard to write my story. It costs me and it still hurts after all these years. It also hurts knowing the judgments and criticism and lack of love I have experienced since telling my story in the church. It was a return to the way I felt as a child when I could not be okay in other people's eyes. People did not understand, nor did they seem to value me enough to try. I still feel that painful wounding today. The approval and acceptance of other people has been too important to me. But I have pushed on, making it a question of "Do we believe the Gospel or not?" I have challenged many to hear me out and extend the Gospel to me. I had to first receive and believe Christ myself to do this!

One of the hardest, if not the hardest thing in life for me was to finally admit the truth to myself and stop hiding. I found it so difficult to face myself and my sin and then to tell others what I have done and who I have been. I came to understand the heart of God toward me so that I could live the Gospel to myself in authenticity. It was an impossible task until I came to embrace my need for Jesus and his work and covenant.

The second hardest issue for me was to acknowledge and process what was done to me and by whom and to forgive them and myself fully. Forgiveness is hard—both accepting it and extending it. It brought me to the end of my abilities. My efforts failed me and I found myself continually repenting of my inability to do what needed done and calling out for mercy.

I came to understand that this is real Christianity. My powerlessness and hopelessness forced me to depend on Christ to do what needed done in me. (This is the secret! Exchanging my powerlessness for God's power; dependence on God to do what I could not do!) I could not accomplish it. (The secret again. My inability, my hopelessness for His ability, His Hope; it took faith and faith pleases God.) My job was to admit the trash, the garbage of sin: my hate and unforgiveness for myself and my husband and others, especially when I felt I wanted to die, or was full of anger and unbelief. I told God repeatedly of my struggles, my pain, why I felt what I felt and I cried out for mercy and worked to believe God for all that I needed. I did not do it perfectly by any means, but God's grace was with me, despite me, and God gave me what I needed. The Gospel lived out in my life: losing my life to gain Christ.

Now I have come to love the Lord and depend on Him and feel His unconditional love for me. I want to obey God and I have set man's approval into God's hands. My husband and I have faced our decision and we know Christ has forgiven us. We have forgiven each other. So I press on with boldness to do as He leads and as His Word instructs me. I relate to this quote by Francis Frangipane: "To inoculate me from the praise of man, He baptized me in the criticism of man, until I died to the control (opinions) of man[16]."

THE CIRCLES OF STORY

Youth for Christ (YFC) uses a picture of three intersecting circles in a triangle, almost like the Olympic rings, to represent the importance of "three stories." This symbol is meant to help us remember that "God's Story, My Story, and Their Story[17]" all connect and intertwine. This is a way of seeing how our relationships with God and others can be connected and grow—a perspective on how to live our hope. The three story elements are evident, repeatedly, in Paul's life and writings. Though sometimes it is long and detailed, and sometimes it is short and to the point, each time Paul clearly tells Christ's story, his personal story, and then relates those stories to the unsaved person. He is a good model to follow as we learn to tell our story. Paul even suggested that we follow his example. "Brethren, be followers together of me, and mark them which walk so as ye have us for an ensample" (Philippians 3:17, KJV).

In Matthew Henry's commentary, he explains,

> "He warns them against following the examples of seducers and evil teachers. (See Philippians 3:18-19.) Many walk, of whom I have told you often, and now tell you weeping, that they are the enemies of the cross of Christ. Observe. There are many called by Christ's name who are enemies to Christ's cross, and the design and intention of it. Their walk is a surer evidence what they are than their profession. By their fruits you shall know them, Matt. 7:20...."[18]

THE ADVENTURE OF HOPE

What a grand privilege to live boldly in this adventure of hope. Paul couldn't walk away from an opportunity to share. Paul had seen Christ and His Kingdom. He embraced Christ and lived with passion and turned the world upside down.

When Paul met Jesus, he became an obedient believer on the spot. He started living his new life immediately, preaching about radically turning to God. He spoke and wrote his clear testimony in Jerusalem and most of the known world. His written words have reached millions for centuries. We are to follow his example. If God handpicked a religious zealot, murderer, and persecutor of believers, God is also willing to save anyone and work through them—including me. We must go out with this Good News. We have the secret of hope for the world.

Peter's Story

After Christ had restored him, Peter led the Pentecost revival where 3000 repented and received forgiveness and new life. Some of these people were present at Christ's crucifixion. They called for and participated in the murder of Messiah. Christ forgave them and saved them. Forgiving murder is the Gospel. Christ forgave them of betraying and crucifying Him. He asked His Father to forgive them and us, and the Father grants forgiveness for the sake of His Son's great sacrifice.

Peter understood that he was no different than those who murdered Christ. He had faced himself, his failures, his sins, his worst moments of life, and had lived to be reunited in grace by Christ. The greatness of the gift of salvation and the experience of grace compelled Peter to want salvation and grace for all. Peter proclaimed the Gospel by the power of the Holy Spirit and not in his own strength. Peter was converted from self-works to Holy Spirit life through his restoration by Christ. I believe Christ longs to bring each of us to this place of conversion. Conversion results in grace empowerment where we will show our love for Christ and feed His sheep by His Spirit, with His truth and love bringing others to the cross where redemption waits for them.

In Acts 2, we read how Peter spoke and preached Christ to the same people who called for Christ's crucifixion. His sermon was powerful and brought conviction to the people there.

Bob Deffinbaugh wrote,

> "Let us remember that this sermon was delivered by a divinely-energized Peter, who now boldly warns those who several weeks earlier had taken part in the crucifixion of the Lord Jesus. He warns them that the day of divine judgment is near, and yet he gives hope because there is still an opportunity for repentance, salvation, and divine blessing. Let us listen well to these words, bearing in mind that thousands came to faith through this sermon."[19]

THE GREATEST HOPE

Peter's message was about hope. They had crucified the Messiah, but there was hope of mercy and compassion—through repentance. God is merciful and delights to show mercy—and forgiveness. How loving, how gracious and merciful. How Jesus. How full of hope is the salvation message!

Lehman Strauss, a pastor and teacher of Old Testament history, wrote,

> "Let us begin at the cross where God begins with it, not with the bloodiness and brutality of the crucifixion, but in the glorious, infinite heights of the foreknowledge of God. Sinners are not saved because their emotions are aroused through hearing about the cruelty of the crucifixion. We are saved by the voluntary, vicarious death of the eternal Son of God, who knew that He was coming to die in our place. 'Even as the Son of man came not to be ministered unto, but to minister, and to give his life a ransom for many'" (Matthew 20:28).[20]

Here we see the miracle of hope.

Peter is a hero to me. He and his story give me hope in my hopeless places. He knew hopelessness in himself and gained hope in Christ.

I have known failure and hopelessness in myself and my performance. Perhaps you have too. I have not wanted to fail Christ and have prided myself in my works and performances, yet in the end I have denied Christ repeatedly for being ashamed to boast on His work on my behalf in giving testimony of His forgiveness through my story. No more. I will boast of Christ. God can surely use the ugliest sins of my life to bring Him glory. There is no room for pride, only awe. The secret of the Lord is with me because I fear God, and He has shown me His covenant. Praise His name.

Jesus is the greatest hero. He gave His all, His very life and still makes heroes out of those who deny him, betray or sin again him. Heroes after failure! What love, what loyalty, what hope He gives! (Finish paragraph with the sentence that is there:) Do you see this? God used Peter's story to bring me hope. And He can do the same with your story for other people.

A RE-DO

Most of us would love to have our worst moments and our most shameful sins and guilt erased instead of exposed. We would love to be given a complete re-do. Imagine that all the degrading things you have ever said or done could be eliminated from the record of God. Seems impossible.

But what is impossible with man is possible with God. Not only can we be forgiven, but God will use our bad for good in God's Kingdom—as promised in Romans 8:28. We cannot earn or produce our re-do. Christ's forgiveness and His promised new life give new opportunities even though we have failed.

Christ died so you might be forgiven, freed, saved, not condemned—and your story will be nestled in His story so others can come to know Christ. He wants us to have the re-do. Christ came for us to be saved—reborn. This re-do begins with repentance, Jesus' call to each of us and the first words of His earthly ministry were "Follow Me" (Matthew 4:17). Following begins with repentance, which means a 180-degree turn: we were going our own way, but now we are choosing His way. Repentance is a gift of immeasurable richness and is necessary for salvation and for our onward journey to be more like Christ. It is death to sin, to our lust and fleshly nature, and saying yes to His will. We receive forgiveness through repentance and then choose to cooperate with His Spirit for true revival.

In that revival, God chooses to use the ugliest parts of our story for His glory.

PETER'S STORY: WHAT CAN WE LEARN?

Peter's story is a great example of a re-do. He had denied Christ and defiantly gone his own way. But when he repented, he turned again, to strengthen his brethren, as Jesus said he would (Luke 22:32). Jesus restored Peter, gracing him with compassion, humility, mercy, forgiveness, reconciliation, and restoration. Peter's life was re-framed for God's Kingdom and He shone Christ's Light. He was released from his failure to proclaim the Gospel. Peter was converted by the experience of grace and the Spirit's work in him empowered his works. (Ephesians 2:10).

GO TELL THE WORLD

Jesus gave the Great Commission, telling us to go to the world. (See Matthew 28.) My story and your story have the power to open the eyes of others. When we tell our story, we reveal the differences between dark and light, and we can help people to choose light—Christ. If I tell about my past life of darkness and sin, it is not for shock value nor do I tell it to glorify the darkness. My story simply shows that I was a sinner, but because Christ entered my life, I am forgiven, and I am reborn. Christ brought light, life, and hope. Telling our story presents Christ's offer of forgiveness to all who will believe.

In his devotional *We Are Butterflies*, Neil Anderson helped me to see that healing is not found only in receiving forgiveness for sin, but in the living from the new heart and life position as Christ's bride. Paul wrote, "For it is God who is at work in you, both to will and to work for His good pleasure. Yes, to know Christ is eternal life but to live for and with Him as King and us in relationship to Him as His Bride, His Beloved is our hope, confidence and joy" (Philippians 2:13).

Our behavior, thinking, and self-perception is changed by our relationship and position in Christ. Anderson says, "we are not redeemed caterpillars; we are butterflies. Why would you want to crawl in some false humility when you are called to mount up with wings as eagles?" He continues, "Humility is not putting yourself down when God is trying to build you up. Self-abasement has the appearance of wisdom, but it has no value against fleshly indulgence according to Colossians 2:23. Humility is confidence properly placed. We need to be like Paul and 'put no confidence in the flesh' Philippians 3:3." He admonishes us to "put our confidence in God and reminds us that God is at work in us as Philippians 2:13 promises."

RICHES BEYOND COMPARE

A certain Civil War veteran lived like a vagabond, yet he was well known for talking about President Lincoln as his friend. Despite his banged-up, beggar-like life, he incessantly spoke of the beloved president as his friend. People were skeptical of his relationship with the president because of his status in life. Someone asked him to prove he knew President Lincoln. The man took out a much-folded paper from his old wallet. Apparently he could not read, so he had never read what his paper said, but a bystander declared that the paper he carried with him was a generous Lincoln-signed federal pension. He no longer had to walk around like a poor beggar! President Lincoln had made him rich with all kinds of provisions for a great life![21]

Christ has made Christians rich with a new life, yet the enemy has often hindered or deceived us to feel or live like paupers––like the elephant, chained to nothing. We are to live and discover the riches Christ secured for us.

The key to victory is faith, taking God at His Word and acting on what He says. We have access to Christ and His promises, and we must use God's truths to capitalize on what Christ has already done. As we read our Bibles, what the word of God actually says, we see that we are not paupers. Instead we can cash in on His great salvation, and boldly tell of the riches that overcame our previous poverty.

"In Christ, we have every spiritual blessing" (Ephesians 1:3).

"We are complete in Christ" (Colossians 2:10).

These declarations mean that we can know and appropriate His blessings. We are not to live in the mindset of the kingdom of the shackle any longer.

UNMASKING THE ELEPHANT

It is a stop-in-your-tracks moment when you realize most of your life has been a lie, and to discover that you didn't know the level of deception you were living under. It is a turn-around moment when you realize how much power those lies had over you. Now I wonder how it took me so long to come to this realization. Was I indoctrinated so thoroughly and effectively that I did not know truth from lies? Yes. Did I know the power of a lie? No, I did not. Are there others who are living just as I was living? I think so.

Christ calls us to live real in our redemption by first knowing truth and then by facing our pasts in honesty. When we apply the truth of the Gospel to our lives, we are able to share my story to show God's story of hope and the splendor of grace in the work of Christ on my behalf.

We can live the life of hope.

This is unmasking the elephant: being honest with the secrets and shame that have kept us shackled. Can it expose us to the censure and condemnation of other people? Yes. But the true purpose of being forthright with our stories, even though it requires great boldness and at times can cause us great pain, is to bring salvation's message of healing and provide the opportunity for God to glorify Himself through His work in the darkest parts of our lives. Then, and only then, will we walk in true freedom. Then, and only then, will we live in the fullness of the riches Christ's cross bought for us and for others!

REDEMPTION

Because the Lord works all things together for good for us who love Him, we have assurance that whatever we have done, whatever we were victims of, can be used to bring about good. The terrible events of my first 21 years of life are turning into good pictures of God's redemption. Because I am so convinced of God's Work on my behalf—His purchasing my redemption—I am able to share my story. God exchanges the horrible for the wonderful and amazing through Jesus. Where else can you take your rags and receive riches? Your lies are exchanged for His truth at His cross.

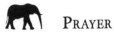 ## PRAYER

Dear LORD, it hurts to reveal our secrets; to own up to the ways we have fallen short. But, Father, we recognize that our stories do not end with our failure; they end with the hope of a new heart, forgiveness, and exchanging our weakness for your strength and eternal life. In you, we have a re-do. In you, we are no longer paupers, but children of a King, who have access to riches beyond compare. Let us allow you the opportunity to glorify yourself through our stories by unmasking our elephants and opening ourselves to your healing, allowing you to use the story you are writing in us as a tool to bring others to you. In Christ's precious name, amen.

PART 2:
ELEPHANT STAMPEDE

The elephants had been a tranquil, majestic, massive part of the scenery outside the little village. The peace was broken, however—perhaps by a loud noise nearby, or some other perceived threat—and the herd went from peaceful grazing to full-throttle stampede in the matter of moments. Suddenly, they were destroying everything around them, trampling, rushing, and raging. They were uncontrollable, unstoppable. Usually harmless, now their heavy feet destroyed everything in their way, trampling everything smaller, quieter, and less fortunate.

The usually gentle creatures now caused injury and death and loss out of fear and carelessness. Or perhaps they caused this destruction as a result of ignorance, since what they feared was no actual "threat" after all.

In some cases, this is a sad image of the church and its response to the shackled elephants among us. Instead of seeing people, hurting and broken, so often we see just the vile sin and the labels that go with it—not unlike how people who knew the Samaritan woman would have seen her. And so in our stampede against the threat of sin, which Christ has already defeated, we trample to death the little broken ones who have been damaged by it already. Damaged by the abuse, by the secrets and shame and the shackles that have imprisoned them for so long. We don't often choose the response of love and Gospel truth that would lead them toward freedom.

I hope in this section to do two things—first of all, to encourage shackled elephants that there is more to the Gospel than a stampede. We don't have to join the trampling herd! And second of all, I want to awaken the Body of Christ to the impact that our actions have in the world, whether for good by drawing the shackled elephants toward heralding the Gospel as we are all called to do, or for evil, by a laissez faire approach to sin and sinners that causes misperceptions of the Gospel... or worse.

6

THE CHURCH NEEDS HOPE

And now these three remain: faith, hope, and love. But the greatest of these is love. (1 Cor 13:13, NET)

"There is a difference between knowing the path and walking the path." Morpheus, The Matrix

Many things are possible for the person who has hope. Even more is possible for the person who has faith. And still more is possible for the person who knows how to love. But everything is possible for the person who practices all three virtues. (Brother Lawrence)

Today I received two phone calls, both from close friends. The first caller shared a prayer need for a man struggling with bisexuality and drug use. "This man is so easy to love," she said.

I felt myself bristle and was surprised by my silent reaction. I asked myself and the Lord why.

As I learned more about the man, I discovered that he is open about his sin and knows it is sin, yet he had been continuing in it. He is accepted, cared about, and loved by Christians who pray for him and tell him the true Gospel and the truth of its transforming power. Committed Christians, sold out to the great salvation they have experienced, are ministering to him and allowing him to confess his sins to them—without judging him. (Galatians 6:1; Matthew 18:15; Matthew 7:1; Romans 14:13.) They hold him accountable, confront him in love, discipline but do not reject or attack his character. Instead, they show Him Christ's grace and kindness, which often lead to true repentance.

"This young man would not step foot in a conventional church," my friend told me. "He knows his shame and would not venture where more shame would be given. He wants his freedom, so he has made the personal decision to just leave his sin at the cross. I'm thankful too that there are places for him to go and not receive condemnation, but rather truth and a way to freedom."

I realized that I felt jealous. I have rarely, if ever, had this kind of love in the Christian community. In fact, more than one pastor has wounded me greatly in my process of trying to get spiritual help when I shared my history. Even though I had cleaned up, was no longer living that way and was trying to serve God, I was often rejected, treated as an outcast, and hurt deeply once my past was known. I have renounced my sexual sins and am living as close to Christ as I know how—but still I have been unaccepted by most in the church. Those shackles: "Why am I not lovable? What is wrong with me? Where is God?" try to return. It takes effort to have my identity in Christ, the Gospel and love of God be my standard instead of the way people treat me.

I still have the fleshly tendency to tell myself I am better than that bisexual young man, because I have been living a pure life. After prayer and further reflection, however, I decided to rejoice that the Gospel of hope and truthful, unconditional love is being lived out to this young man. My prayer is that he will be so overcome by the love of Christ and the love of Christ's followers, that he will allow the Holy Spirit to completely break the shackle of his same-sex attraction.

The second phone call was a dear friend on missionary assignment. She said that she had shared with her mission co-workers a copy of the newspaper editorial she felt led to write years ago that gave testimony of her abortion.

Her fellow missionaries received and loved her. I rejoiced at how they are living the Gospel in response to her. I remembered when she shared the rejection, the shunning, and the outright meanness she experienced from many in the so-called Christian community after this editorial came out initially. She was treated like a leper. Now though, I praised God for the love these other missionaries had shown her.

True Gospel-living Christians exist! They are the ones who embrace the sinner, but speak out against the sin only as the Holy Spirit leads. Tragically, there are many that have been hurt by legalism in the church, or those who speak out in hatred but somehow "on God's behalf." The true church is supposed to be a hospital for the sin-sick, where they can find the answer for their sin and the power to overcome it.

UNACCEPTED

For years some church leaders outright discouraged me from telling my story. I was told, "It is under the blood. Never speak of it again." Believers who knew the extent of my story often treated me with what I perceived as judgment and contempt. I would suddenly be avoided, talked about, sneered at, held back, not allowed to teach, or completely ignored. Being invisible, feeling like I did not exist, was sometimes the worst rejection. This was my elephant stampede: my woundedness further trampled by those I was supposedly to have trusted.

My courage has been challenged as I have struggled to be received and accepted by the church. Telling "the world" how God has forgiven and transformed me has been much easier than telling my story to the "churched."

I had wanted to be good so I would be loved. I did not fully realize that Christ loves me, even when I am bad—and that as His follower, I am to extend that same grace to others. Most of my life, I received conditional love and did not understand what unconditional love offers.

I developed a wrong perception about the church, too. I do love and respect every teacher I have ever had. I have been blessed by strong, mature, scholarly teachers. I recognize that my feelings of shame may have kept me from recognizing the love they offered. But it seemed that often they taught biblical love with their words, but I rarely felt accepted and loved by their actions.

I spent hours each day reading and meditating on God's Word. I tried to share what I'd learned with excitement and—I'll admit—sometimes with pride. Sadly. I worked to be accepted but rarely was, no matter how hard I did work! So in all this mess, even with my desire to do right and trying to do right, I was sometimes wrong. Feeling worthless but trying to prove myself was a lifestyle. It stunk.

I felt unaccepted, unloved, and inferior—repeating my childhood feelings without realizing it. And the more unaccepted I felt, the more worthlessness I sensed (real or not); these feelings fueled my efforts to try harder to be accepted and to be lovable. The harder I tried, the more pride I fought and the more rejection I received. It was a vicious cycle, yet I was unaware of it at the time. Looking back, I see my selfish role in those feelings of rejection. Performing for love is a trap and miserable pit. Wanting and waiting for others' affirmations is a setup for disappointment and disillusionment. It could have led me to death by suicide had not the Lord kept me.

I finally became aware of and got sick of my own hypocrisy. I had not understood myself or what drove me for the longest time. I blamed the leaders of the church because they didn't seem to love me unconditionally. I often felt more love from unbelievers.

During these long hours reading the Word, I came to know the Lord more closely, even if my motives were more selfish than not. Thankfully with Jesus I can be my true self, and He loves me unconditionally. If my heart condemns me, God is greater than my heart and knows all things (1 John 3:20). God showed me my part in the rejections and I repented. Repentance is a true gift!

THE CHURCH NEEDS HOPE

Why does the church often respond badly to the confession of sin? There are scores like me and like my missionary friend who have either had an abortion or suffered abuse and its effects.

Jesus restored people like us with gentleness, yet the church community often leaves us in our perpetual pain, rejecting us because of our past. I have done my own share of wounding others too! I am not out to bash the church. I am just as guilty.

Many of us, some without even realizing it, have often been brutal and unloving to large groups of people or individuals: the victims of elephants in the room. Many church members just don't know how to deal with the people or issues seen as threatening to church life as we know it, things that "aren't safe." It is our sin of omission: we have not extended the Gospel or loved as Jesus loves. And what we omit or neglect or forget to do can be a trampling force that crushes the spirits of the shackled and the way they perceive the Body of Christ.

We as believers need to repent of our failure to make His true Gospel—a grace-based, love-oriented story of acceptance and transformation—our main message and lifestyle. We need to love, understand, be compassionate, serve, and get the word out to these millions that God is gracious and forgives. Our lives need to show we know Christ and His forgiveness and grace. The work of the cross brought forgiveness. The miracle of resurrection proved mercy triumphed over judgment.

We who were shackled elephants do not need to join the stampede. Those who may be realizing now that you are part of the stampede—could that, for you, be a shackle?

Discouraging Trends

In my years, I have seen many churches that do not present the true Gospel and follow the Holy Spirit for living. I have observed some discouraging trends.

- Many are not taught to understand the doctrine of depravity or the incredible solution found in the greatness of what Christ did for us.
- Some are not taught to love Jesus or hear Him.
- Most are taught rules to follow instead of a Savior to love.
- Many are not taught the bare basics of the Gospel with a solid foundation.
- A good number depend on "self" and not the Holy Spirit.

We are a mess, and we need a revolution of the true Gospel so we can worship in spirit and in truth. We need eyes to see as our Lord sees.

HOPE FOR VICTIMS OF SEXUAL ABUSE

What if we saw survivors of abuse the way God sees them?

Sexual abuse survivors need the body of Christ to come alongside and love them unconditionally, to minister the true Gospel of grace and connect them to the true love of Christ. They can know Christ and thrive with His Spirit. They need to know that there will be an eternal vindication and justice. God knows and will respond. There are great needs during recovery. Healing happens when we learn and apply the real Gospel.

By following Christ we replace lies with truth, choose forgiveness and love (the cross), and follow the ways of Christ. Gospel becomes our very lives and recovery. Unloving, judgmental stances that are inconsistent with the true love of Christ hinder salvation, recovery, and freedom. If the church does not return to Christ and His true Gospel, upholding His word, our testimony may be lost.

NEW CREATION AND BRIDGE BUILDER

Only the Spirit of God convicts a soul. We are to pray and to speak truth in love. We should state our convictions and stand for life—in love. The rest is in His hands. It isn't my job to convict people. Stating our convictions and bringing people to conviction are different! I pray and trust God because it's not about who's right and who's wrong. As a Christ follower, my goal must be to care about the person and his or her eternal soul exactly the same way Christ cares.

It is time that we build a bridge to those in the midst of these issues—those who have had an abortion, for instance, even if he or she still maintains their pro-choice stance. There are many who have had one or more abortions and do not think it is wrong at all.

Think about it. Abortion is legal, and our culture paints positive pictures of being pro-choice, so there is little reason for any unbeliever who has had an abortion to feel guilty or uncomfortable about the choice they made. Some are not bothered by it and feel there is nothing to forgive.

One friend told me that prior to accepting Christ as her Savior, she had had two abortions. She told me that the two abortions played no part in her decision to accept Christ because she had had no guilt, negative feelings, or convictions about them. After she was saved, though, The Lord brought her to a realization of the enormity of her decisions. Then she felt sorrow. She asked the Lord for forgiveness and healing regarding these abortions. The Lord brought her to this healing place—it did not happen as a result of the accusation or condemnation of anyone else. Bringing conviction is the Holy Spirit's role, not ours.

Awake, O Sleeper!

In the book *I Saw the Lord*, Anne Graham Lotz boldly suggests that the church needs to repent. She writes, "After the horrific devastation of 9/11, many church leaders were pointing their fingers at national and social sins as a reason for what they saw as God's judgment on our nation. Abortion on demand and the broad acceptance of homosexuality were the grievous sins most commonly noted. But I could not help wondering if the Son of God was focused on His own people, the church, with eyes like blazing fire and feet like burnished bronze."[22]

She gives a passionate plea for us to consider just how far we have come from the cross, which is the power to change lives. She writes that we are "a people loaded with guilt because while we have a form of godliness we deny the power of the cross…. The church often has not established a personal relationship with God through faith in Jesus Christ. We have conformed more to the world and have forsaken the Lord by turning our back on Him so often!"[23]

I agree with her. The church is guilty, and I have also been guilty. We must change our focus and message from self to Jesus and His saving work—His Gospel. We need a wake-up call. God has awakened me and there are many who are also awake. I am grateful and encouraged by those who are living and heralding the Gospel.

Jesus has done for me what He did for the woman at the well, and He has been very real to me in this process. Jesus is the best part of my life, the best gift, and the best treasure.

The Lord pursued Adam in the garden. He did not wait until Adam cleaned himself up. He offered the cover. We must give this gift of life message, Christ's atoning cover, to others so eternal death will pass them over. Christ died for us while we were His enemies, and in sin. He rose so we could live eternally.

Focusing on the Problem

One Sunday in 2013, I attended a church service that coincided with the 40th anniversary of the Roe v. Wade decision. The sermon was full of biblical truths on the wages of sin, especially abortion—and yet lacked a clear message of the mercy of God.

Focusing on the sinfulness of abortion is effective in showing us the forgiveness we truly need, but, in my opinion, leaves the listener (particularly a listener with a heavy conscience) with no hope and a mountain of shame. This is devastating, and fails to complete the story by proclaiming the goodness of God and His offer of forgiveness of all sins through Christ Jesus. Salvation is offered by what Jesus has done. Because I felt the focus was only on the magnitude of the sin, omitting the grace of God, I left that church utterly devastated. I am sure that I was not alone, and that there were others who needed to hear the message of mercy!

Jesus gives hope and help to people in need. Needy ones long to feel loved unconditionally. Jesus poured Himself out for us in amazing grace and unmerited favor and mercy. His work was not in vain. Salvation is for any who will believe regardless of their past. We must teach truth covered in love. Presenting the problem without the solution brings shame, condemnation, and hopelessness. Why is the message of grace and mercy through the work of Christ on the cross not clearly proclaimed in every church today?

Jesus is truth and grace. Sometimes, though, we forget to include grace. Theology, law, and rules are taught, but not grace or mercy. Living in this atmosphere causes us to hide our sin, instead of repenting and thus accepting the free gift of forgiveness. The blood of Christ and His broken body are precious. The gift of forgiveness is readily available at the cross and must be heralded. We need not try to cover our sin with good works. "Truth without grace is brutality and grace without truth is hypocrisy."[24]

CALLED TO HERALD, NOT TO HINDER

During a spinal surgery in December of 2012, I had an experience with the Lord. It is hard to put in words what I experienced. When I woke up after the surgery, I had a sure knowledge that God is angry at those of His people who are not making the message of Jesus, His shed blood, and death on the cross for the atonement of sins the main message of their lives. I knew He was calling me to first repent and then sound the alarm on this heinous sin of not heralding the true Gospel.

God is not pleased if we diminish the cross of Christ and the majesty and great sacrifices of Christ. I knew that Jesus had died for me because I had been guilty, and maybe was still guilty, of being a hypocrite and blocking others from reaching the cross and a new life in Christ through my own religiosity.

I turned to the Lord with repentance, reverence and fierce determination to obey Him. The Lord was clearly calling me to boast on Christ and give my testimony. I was sobered and seriously affected by this experience.

We will discuss heralding the Gospel more in the next section, but it is important to reiterate this: we cannot herald the Gospel, or represent it well to others, if we are ourselves missing the true Gospel of Jesus Christ. It is my hope that we will place our faith only in Christ's work, and then consistently live the Gospel out in day-to-day life, within our family and within the church. I do not want to live religiously, self-righteously, unloving, or unforgiving. Not one more day. I want to give grace. I want to live in victory.

 ## PRAYER

Dear Father, help us to become more like your Son Jesus, like He was with the woman at the well—more loving, accepting and merciful yet bringing people to the truth by kindness, compassion, and a gracious Spirit. Give us forgiving hearts and make us bridge builders boasting on the cross of Christ as we give our testimony. Help us love the rejected, those whom others have given up on, and those who are outcasts. Let us share your Gospel in spirit and in truth so people receive living water. Help us be humble and Christlike. Thank you for your example and forgiveness and the hope that it brings. Keep changing us, LORD. All our hope is in you. In Jesus' name, amen.

GOSPEL OF HOPE

Brethren, my heart's desire and my prayer to God for them is for their salvation. For I testify about them that they have a zeal for God, but not in accordance with knowledge. For not knowing about God's righteousness and seeking to establish their own, they did not subject themselves to the righteousness of God. For Christ is the end of the law for righteousness to everyone who believes (Romans 10:1-4, NASB).

For it is by grace you have been saved, through faith – and this is not from yourselves, it is the gift of God (Ephesians 2:8, NIV).

Let your unfailing love surround us, LORD, for our hope is in you alone (Proverbs 31:22, NLT)

"Mark what I say again. You may know a good deal about Christ, by a kind of head knowledge. You may know who He was, and where He was born, and what He did. You may know His miracles, His sayings, His prophecies, and His ordinances. You may know how He lived, and how He suffered, and how He died. But unless you know the power of Christ's cross by experience—unless you know and feel within that the blood shed on that cross has washed away your own particular sins—unless you are willing to confess that your salvation depends entirely on the work that Christ did upon the cross—unless this be the case, Christ will profit you nothing. The mere knowing Christ's name will never save you. You must know His cross, and His blood, or else you will die in your sins."—JC Ryles

The big church was packed to overflowing at the funeral of a long-time family friend. I felt sad that he was so young and died so tragically. My sadness extended to his family, our community, our church, and America. *So much at stake, so much lost.*

The service beautifully honored the family and the deceased, speaking of God's Word, including Jesus's death and resurrection. But then the pastor said: "I believe if our friend could speak to us, his message would be 'be good.'"

I thought that he may have said those words as a warning to us, because it is true that not living righteously has its negative consequences. We are to respect God's laws and obey them for our own good. They are made to protect us, not steal from us. Following the law does not save us eternally, though it does save us from the earthly consequences of wrong choices.

But even if that was the pastor's intent, he never finished the story. Jesus and His death and resurrection were spoken about, yes, but the need for Jesus, and the fact that we can never make it on our own by our own goodness or works, was not discussed at all the whole service.

I realized then that in order for us to understand what the true Gospel is and how it impacts our lives, we have to understand what it *isn't*. Too much damage is done in churches, both to believers and to nonbelievers, when the Gospel itself, the core of our faith, is misrepresented. This is what sets the elephants stampeding.

"Be good" is not the message of the Good News. The Gospel message is "Jesus is good." Jesus is God; He took our *not-good*, sin, so we could be made *good*, righteous in Him through faith. It is all the work of God and not of man. Man cannot earn salvation; God alone accomplishes it.

POWERLESS WITHOUT CHRIST

When I was swimming competitively, we often heard our coach screaming at us: "Don't ever say 'I can't!'" If we whined that we couldn't do the training, we were assigned extra laps and other work as a consequence of our unbelief in our abilities.

But as it usually does, the Kingdom turns this concept on its head. Yes, God has showered you with abilities and talents, but He wants you to allow Him to use them through you. Our works do not save us but are evidence of our salvation; an outworking of God's Spirit and the power of His Spirit at work through us that we are priviledged to harness. Without His Spirit nothing can be accomplished eternally. "Without Him we can do nothing" John 15:5 is my life verse. I used to "cringe" at that verse. Now I see the value and cherish the verse as the privledge it is and the honor it is for Christ to work in and through me.

When we surrender to Him and do as He leads, giving up trying to do it all alone, we find His yoke is easy. (Matthew 11:30) Ironically, I find this one of the hardest verses in the Bible to really live.

I am powerless to change myself from the inside out. I have had to plead for God to do what only He can do. And He has. And is. I am learning to depend on God to change me and I seek Him to accomplish what needs done in me to experience the Gospel exchange. It is not always easy to admit my sinful thoughts, but God already knows. And the sooner I stop pretending and take it all to Him, the greater the relief and the less I suffer. The Lord has been so gracious and merciful and faithful to me. He has brought me to trust Him and depend more fully on Him daily. How thankful I am.

In my heart, I know I'm doing everything I can to recover from the multiple sexual abuses, my own sexual sins, occult abuse, abortion, church judgments, and the post-traumatic effects on me. I am different from many who have had an abortion. I wanted our baby. I desperately tried to fight for her or him. I gave in to it out of fear and intimidation and other sad reasons too great and lengthy to explain in these pages. But God in His mercy has forgiven me! I have forgiven myself, my husband, and others in order to make peace with myself, my past, and my God. I have repeatedly, confessed, repented, renounced, and prayed the Scriptures. I have prayed and others have prayed for me, too. I've had years of counseling. I've prayed as a family intercessor, breaking generational curses. And I have come to the conclusion that even after I've done all I know to do, I cannot fully and completely accomplish what is needed. But God continues His work, doing what only He does best.

I am powerless, but God has the power. This is the secret of hope. My powerlessness for God's power. Understanding my weakness to overcome is the beginning of finding the secret of hope. Where I can't, God can. Where I am hopeless to accomplish His will, He will do it through me. He is my hope. Last night my husband and I watched a Billy Graham video. Dr. Graham said, "you cannot change your past but you can change your destiny. God can change your past. He can forgive all you have ever done."

Another of Billy Graham's quotes: "Salvation is always 'good news.' It is news of God's love and forgiveness—adoption into His family— fellowship with His people—freedom from the penalty of sin— liberation from the power of sin. Salvation is an act of God. It is initiated by God, wrought by God, and sustained by God." That's the true Gospel.

Conversion from our self-pride and dependence on works of the law is a work of God's Grace. An increase in the grace and wisdom of God upon our lives comes by the Spirit of God working to bring us into all truth and obedience. John the Baptist said, "He must increase, but I *must* decrease" (John 3:30).

GALATIANS "GOSPEL"

I spent way too much time trying to earn my salvation in my own strength. "Be good to be loved" was my heart cry. But this is the works Gospel, which I call the Galatians "Gospel," and it is part of my story that has never been satisfying or effective. I believe it is a "believing, obeying-to-be saved lifestyle" that the circumcision group of Paul's day lived.

At times, the works Gospel gives a false sense of self-assurance and goodness. But this ideology depends on self for righteousness, and not Christ. The works Gospel hinders the true Gospel. Paul says it is cursed and that many are deceived by it, relying on their own righteousness to save.

> *Let God's curse fall on anyone, including us or even an angel from heaven, who preaches a different kind of Good News than the one we preached to you. I say again what we have said before: If anyone preaches any other Good News than the one you welcomed, let that person be cursed. For I would have you know, brothers, that the Gospel that was preached by me is not man's Gospel. For I did not receive it from any man, nor was I taught it, but I received it through a revelation of Jesus Christ (Galatians 1:8-9, 11-12, NLT).*

Paul knew the Galatians were missing the true Gospel because they were trying to gain their salvation by the things they did—just as Paul had done until God mercifully opened his eyes.

The Mystery of Messiah

God's plan has always included His sacrifice, rather than the mere fulfillment of the Law; it was, is, and will always be *grace*. The Lamb was slain before the foundations of the world (Revelation 13:8). God gave the Law to Moses to demonstrate the way to live and to govern social, civil, and spiritual activities. But the Law was never meant to be the sole focus. The Jews became extreme Law followers by adding hundreds of regulations and rules. They thought that if you could follow the Law perfectly, you could reach God. In doing so, they took their eyes off of God. Romans 8. God gave the law for our good but He knew we would not be able to keep the whole of the law because of our sinful nature. We need a Savior. The Messiah. The Law was woven into the salvation plan of God like a mystery—the mystery of Messiah.

When Paul saw Jesus in His glory and power on that Damascus road, he understood the mystery. He had been dead spiritually, steeped in the laws of God, but he did not know God. From that moment on, Paul knew Christ as Lord, and was changed, and salvation power became a reality in his life. The rest of Paul's life heralded the fact that he had experienced the true Gospel: his life was dramatically altered from thinking he had arrived in his self-righteousness (Pharisaism) to living fully in Christ.

Paul realized through that Damascus road experience that even those who have a shameful past have hope.

"We then may know the hope by which He has called us, having the eyes of your hearts enlightened, that you may know what is the hope to which he has called you, what are the riches of his glorious inheritance in the saints (Ephesians 1:18, ESV).

When we turn from sin, confess Christ as Lord, receive His salvation, and surrender to Him, we can know God in the same way Paul did.

One of my greatest realizations, as I have repeated like a broken record, has been that Jesus knows me all the way through and loves me enough to die for me—even before I changed— and He still loves me like this. The next generation needs this message, not a false doctrine or false religion.

MIXED GOSPEL

Many who are born again (saved) are locked in a passionless religious box like the Pharisees. Modeling the Pharisee produces a weakened lifestyle that does little good for anyone. I lived this way for years. A mixture of the two gospels is a power-stealing mix. The power of God at the cross through Christ is the power of the true Gospel. The counterfeit has power that attempts to distort and destroy and thus becomes Satan's greatest threat to the church.

To have the most powerful force on earth available to me but be entrenched in a mixed or false gospel lifestyle is tragic—and life-weakening and God-opposing. I was unaware of how much I was deceived by a works encroachment on the true Gospel in my life. The church environments I had experienced caused me to accept a works mentality apart from the Holy Spirit and that mentality became, for a time, my norm. I believe my experience is a common experience in America.

I so often witness Christian churches, schools, and families teach rules and laws that heap condemnation, shame, works-based principles, and guilt on children. The emphasis on how much Jesus loves and wants a relationship with them, what the cross is, and why it had to be is often either not the main message or missing altogether. What are we doing? Living in grace and faith, running to the cross for forgiveness and overcoming our sins through relationship with Christ by faith—this is the essential Gospel. Anything apart from this is not "Gospel truth" and just leads to more shackles. Are we teaching the Gospel of the Shackled Elephant, or the Good News, the true Gospel of grace where victory, restoration, and overcoming abounds?

Your performance alone, no matter how good it is, cannot please God. God knows our motivations and our hearts. Are you really saved, a true Christian? Or do you just look like one?

A works-based Gospel has no transforming power. If we miss the true Gospel, we will not be able to represent it well, or herald it well, to those around us. A real experience of the power of the true cross of Jesus will replace pre-conceived ideas of Him. It did for me, and has for millions. It is the difference between "false religion dressed in Christianity" and True Gospel Christianity!

FALSE RELIGION VERSUS THE GOSPEL

False religion says, "Be good." Gospel says, "God is good."

False religion says, "My works cancel my sin." Gospel says, "Only Christ's works atone for my sin."

False religion says, "Pay your own way." Gospel says, "Christ paid."

False religion says, "You must earn it." Gospel says, "Receive the gift of grace."

False religion says, "Keep working." Gospel says, "It is finished."

False religion says, "Hide your sin." Gospel says, "Repent and be forgiven."

False religion says, "Big sins can't be redeemed." Gospel says, "All repented sin is redeemed because Christ is the Redeemer who takes all guilt."

False religion says, "I am better than you." Gospel says "We have all sinned and fallen short of the glory of God."

False religion says, "I would never do what you did." Gospel says, "I am no better than anyone, given another's life I could do what they have done."

False religion says, "Compared to you, I'm righteous." Gospel says, "Christ's righteousness is imputed to me."

The list goes on. False religion bashes some sins and exalts others. It believes that depending on grace is too easy or cheap. It perverts the truth, causing people to believe they can do whatever they want—God's forgiveness is sufficient, right? It accepts and exalts temporal pleasure. False religion causes hardheartedness, bitterness, pride, and judgments that wound.

The Gospel, on the other hand, is the repentant sinner being redeemed by Christ alone and indwelt by the Holy Spirit, which results in good works as the fruit of receiving Christ's heartbeat. He took our death. The Gospel brings healing, help, hope, and heaven. It does not boast in its own works, but exalts Christ's work with humility and thanksgiving.

False religion holds us as a captive hostage. The Gospel is truth that sets us free.

JESUS' RESPONSE

In the Gospel of Mark especially, it is evident that Jesus often dealt with the hypocrisy and legalism of religious leaders while He was on earth. He knew hearts. He challenged them with compassion, truth, healing, love, mercy, and grace—and sometimes righteous anger. He was hated by religious leaders for breaking their man-made laws, which were based on their misunderstandings of Torah.

When Jesus seriously dealt with me about my hypocrisy and legalism, He clearly revealed how I had hindered His Gospel and dishonored Him. It grieves me how I have hurt Christ. I do not think I am alone. So many in the church hide behind piety while protecting a putrid past. Instead, we need to show the world what Christ has done for us.

CHRIST ALONE

I discovered that Christ's work on my behalf—and that alone—saves. The true Gospel of Christ alone dramatically changed my life from relying on self to depending on the indwelt Holy Spirit. From living in bondage to living by His mindsets of grace through relationship with Jesus. Without a grace mindset, I tend to look down on others as the first disciples may have looked down on the woman at the well. (See John 4.) A condescending attitude sends people running. It did then and always will. Together may we learn how to change—just as the first disciples learned—from Christ.

Jesus lived love and modeled love for every race, gender, and sinner. Since He is perfect and sinless, He is good—for He truly is God incarnate. He came to earth to save us and lift us up and release us from what holds us down: sin.

GOD CHANGES US

> *For if a man is in Christ he becomes a new person altogether-the past is finished and gone, everything has become fresh and new. (2 Corinthians 5:17, JB Phillips.)*

May God himself, the God who makes everything holy and whole, make you holy and whole, put you together—spirit, soul, and body—and keep you fit for the coming of our Master, Jesus Christ. The One who called you is completely dependable. If he said it, he'll do it! (1 Thessalonians 5:23-24, MSG.)

Clearly, God does a work in us that brings about a dramatic change that we desperately need. He has done it all. He has adopted us into His family and He wants us to start living as members of His family right now. Through the indwelling of His Spirit, He begins to shape us to be the people that we were always meant to be. He patiently molds us through our daily experiences to be more like Jesus. In the process, we can experience a closer relationship with the Father and make Him more the focus of our lives.

He changes us from the worm to the butterfly. We cannot change ourselves. He asks us to stay in His cocoon until He is finished. Our part is to stay with Jesus, under His arm of protection. He is our refuge. The Christian life can seem complicated. But God wants to change our lives.

BUT GOD

The phrase "But God" contains two power-packed words. When my life seems out of control and I see no hope, He steps in and takes control. The greatness of infinite God working on man's behalf to do for man what man could not do. "But God" is to say the impossible becomes possible because of God.

What Jesus has done for me and offers to the world is greater than anything this world offers. This is the story of the Bible and my story, too. God loves us so much that He gave himself to make a way for us to be reconciled to Him and know Him. There is no greater love. (See John 15:13; 1 John 4:8-16.)

NEW FOUNDATION

I eventually experienced a removal from the religious system I was in, and the poison the enemy had tried to plant in me was eradicated. My faith and foundation is now dependent on the finished work of the blood of Jesus Christ in a greater way than it has ever been. It was then that I wanted to do whatever the Lord directed me to do to advance His Kingdom. The greatness of my salvation, through a greater understanding of the cross and resurrection as the fulfillment of God's Covenant transformed me and my faith.

He has surely forgiven me, and it is a happy day when I reflect on the fact that my sins are washed away and I am clean. Most every day I have to remind myself because Satan works relentlessly to try to return me to the feelings of guilt and shame so familiar to me—right back to the elephant shackles. The enemy wants the true Gospel to be hindered. Let us fight him and not each other.

WE CAN KNOW

My husband and I were sitting at our gate in the airport, waiting to board. I felt contemplative, and so I glanced at him, hoping to connect in conversation instead of just staying quiet. "What are you thinking?"

"About this song, actually," he replied.

It was Eric Clapton's "Tears of Heaven," which was written about his young son who died. In the moving lyrics he questioned if they'd be reunited in heaven, longing to see his boy again. He was looking for peace and wondering what eternity held.

I was moved. "How sad," I said. Our story was so different from Eric Clapton's, but our heartache was so similar. We had lost a child, too, and longed to see our baby again in heaven. But I realized, too: We had hope. And I questioned if such a famous songwriter had the same hope we shared. Had the message of hope ever been clearly communicated to him? If so, had he experienced Christ's comfort in his torrential grief and loss? The Gospel is so important, so life giving, so imperative. Do people miss the Gospel by their own choice, or because the messengers are obscure, unclear, and hindering to their message by leaving Christ out of the picture?

We can *know* beyond the shadow of the doubt that the Gospel is true. In 1 John 5:13, the Bible tells us, "These things I have written to you who believe in the name of the Son of God, so that you may *know* that you have eternal life" (emphasis mine). When we believe in His name and the power of His blood shed on the cross, that knowledge and assurance is ours. So is the responsibility to share the truth with others. Even when told the truth, people can still believe lies that then hinder them from receiving the great pardon of forgiveness offered them. For instance, I told my husband about the article I had just read the day before about a man who wrote Billy Graham from prison saying he had gotten mad and killed a man. He asked if God could forgive him. Billy answered yes and explained (as detailed on pages 33 and 36). But what had further shocked me was that underneath Dr. Graham's answer a man had written in "yeah but God is a hypocrite. He will forgive you but you have to give your life to him!" I have thought on this man's comment. A lie that powerful has apparently prevented that man from receiving a great pardon! Lies are destroyers. Lies like: "if we live for God we will live in an inferior way, ie: God holds out on us, God is a taker not a giver." These lies are staggering and as old as the Garden of Eden. People, including myself have believed God's way is not as good or fun, happy or satisfying.... That is why we don't live for God fully at times, these kinds of lies weasle their way too much in place! If we ever showed how good God is and really lived like we believed it, many would want him! We both agreed to the truth of God's goodness and our desire to share the truth of God's love and grace.

That day was a first for me in really *knowing* through shared moments of intimacy with my husband that I had forgiven him from my heart. An experience of a deeper level of forgiveness, resolution and living hope was felt that comforted and brought me peace. We spoke of knowing we will see our child in heaven one day- not because of what we've done, but because of Christ!

THE VICTORY OF THE CROSS

The enemy wants the Gospel not to "feel" true or "be" true to us. He works relentlessly to try to convince us to believe lies like these:

- "You are so sinful that Jesus would not forgive you!"
- "You are actually pretty good in your own right, because you follow all the rules! You don't need the cross."
- "It's just no use —you should just give up trying altogether."
- "I can't do it anymore. Why try. It seems pointless, hopeless."
- "It will never change. What is the value of my surrender or obedience? It doesn't pay. The Gospel doesn't seem to work."

Whatever Satan's ploy, his goal is to diminish the cross and the forgiveness of sins based on Christ's work, because Satan knows the arsenal of God's power for man is at the cross. The greatest reversals are possible there.

The truth: We all are guilty of sin and all need the cross and the Gospel, whether it feels true or not. Satan accuses, condemns, works to deceive, and tries to wreck our faith. He tempts us with things that seem to look good, perverts the grace of God, and tries to sabotage our freedom, especially by weakening our understanding of the cross and its power and victory. He hinders our repentance. He wants us to miss what Christ came to give. He often tries to trap us in our own works or sins and force us back into the bondage of trying to earn our righteousness in our own strength or in lies that say we can never be different.

We do not earn salvation. It depends on Christ alone. Once we know Christ, He abides in us. Our relationship with Him grows as we depend on Him and learn of Him by His Word, prayer, and fellowship. We must preach Jesus alone for salvation.

The two extremes in life—those who think they may be too far gone for God's mercy and those who think they are so good they rely on themselves for salvation—are missing the life of Christ. Both need brought to the cross, where Christ's forgiveness of sins is offered, His lovingkindness is magnified, His mercy meets with justice, and salvation can be received. His grace and glory await.

He loves us right where we are and right as we are. Jesus died while we were still sinners. The greatest place of victory is the cross. The cross brings forth the resurrection and mercy hope. It holds the secret.

Prayer

Dear Heavenly Father, thank you that the victory over sin and death was won by Christ: that He took sin, death, hell, the works of the enemy, and every curse for us. Our sins demanded death. Thank you for paying our debt! Please forgive us your people for living as though we are good enough on our own, which belittles the greatness of the cross and the magnitude of Christ's sacrifice and love. Forgive our pride and ingratitude! Help us to know the true Gospel of grace and abandon the idea that somehow we can be good enough on our own. Because of you, LORD, there is hope. Help us walk worthy of you as we have been called into your Kingdom (1 Thessalonians 2:12). In Jesus' name, amen.

8

HOPE FOR THE CULTURAL COLLISION

"I am the light of the world. The one who follows me will never walk
in darkness, but will have the light of life" (John 8:12, NET).

"Who hath delivered us from the power of darkness, and hath translated
us into the kingdom of his dear Son" (Colossians 1:13, KJV).

"When a newspaper posed the question, 'What's Wrong with the World?' the
Catholic thinker G. K. Chesterton reputedly wrote a brief letter in response:
'Dear Sirs: I am. Sincerely Yours, G. K. Chesterton.'[25]"

"You are the light of the world. A city set on a hill cannot be hidden; nor does anyone
light a lamp and put it under a basket, but on the lampstand, and it gives light to all who
are in the house. Let your light shine before men in such a way that they may see your
good works, and glorify your Father who is in heaven." (Matthew 5:14-16, NASB)

"Jonathan Edwards, in his sermon entitled 'Christian Happiness', said that there are three
reasons why any Christian who knows Christ, and knows they know Christ, can be completely
content and free from worry. The three reasons are: your bad things will turn out for good;
your good things can never be taken away from you; and the best things are yet to come."[26]

It has been called the "greatest sea disaster in history,"[27] and among the worst shark attacks
in history. After delivering the world's first operational atomic bomb to the island of Tinian
in July of 1945, the Navy cruiser *USS Indianapolis* left port in Guam to sail unescorted to the
Philippines. Just a few days later, however, she was torpedoed by a Japanese submarine just a

few minutes after midnight. The torpedoes struck near a fuel tank and a powder magazine, and the second explosion ripped the ship apart. Within minutes she had sunk.

Almost 1,200 sailors had been aboard; it is estimated that 900 made it into the water before she sank. That didn't mean survival for everyone. Shark attacks began before the sun rose the next day, and relentlessly persisted the five days the men were in the water. By the time they were finally accidentally discovered and rescued, only 317 men were still alive. The rest had perished due to the constant shark attacks, lack of food, consumption of saltwater, and exposure.

I see the times we live in today as potentially the "greatest cultural disaster of history"— our situation could be just as devastating as the *Indianapolis* with its consequences and loss of life, if the course we are on is not quickly altered! Our culture as a whole is on a collision course with itself, as it struggles to be accepting of all things, yet rejects the truth and the true love of Jesus. The church today, in this analogy, could be seen as the ship. Our enemy has targeted us with the torpedoes of lies and sin, causing a disastrous conflict that ultimately threatens to sink our ship. If we allow our feelings or the culture to dictate our truth we could sink or be torn asunder by the enemy!

Church culture must not be part of the problem. We must not travel unescorted into enemy waters, and we must be aware of the sharks lurking below the surface. We, as the church, should provide a lifeboat to those who are sinking; a rescue, a refuge and a place of restoration! We carry an atomic bomb, too—the Gospel, which will destroy the enemy's territory, his works, and his schemes, and turn the tide on the spiritual war. But we have to use the armor we've been given and walk in the power of the Holy Spirit. We must use the cross of Christ and the blood of the Lamb as our greatest weapons, living out Revelation 12:11! If we are non-communicative with our "home base" (Christ), we may not fare better than those on the *Indianapolis* that fateful voyage. Our "ship" needs to be ready and vigilant. We need to be prayerful, watchful and abiding in the fullness of the Spirit.

We need to hope in truth, not denial.

We have problems in the church that need addressing. If we do not start addressing the fact that we have not generally made the true Gospel the main event in the church, it could be overtaken by the culture, and the ship of Gospel Truth could go down. Jesus, His cross, death, and resurrection need to be center stage. Culture hides the truth, and many do not want to see or know. But those who are willing can make a difference for life and hope.

CULTURE EXPERIENCES

Our culture is full of sin and darkness. The number of those bound by the chains of pornography, pedophilia, prostitution, sex trafficking, sexual abuse, and sexual sin in general seem to have grown exponentially. As mentioned before, regret of abortion is the most common experience of mankind in our generation.

Christians are often not known for their love or Gospel living. Some who call themselves Christians have hated and bashed those who identify as LGBTQ. At the other extreme are the churches that have openly advanced homosexuals as leaders in the churches. The Word of God is often not upheld, or remains unknown or misconstrued.

The list is endless. Our world, including our spiritual family, needs the love, truth, repentance, forgiveness, grace and mercy found in the real Gospel. God's Word is the foundation we need and Christ is our mainstay. We must herald the real Gospel in the order Paul taught it—"believe, saved, obey"—through the work of Christ (wielding the real sword of the Spirit of God). In this order Christianity is the true religion of the work of God on man's behalf. It is the true secret of hope.

Our world is depending on us living out the message of Hope. The downward spiral of sin is a way of life common in our world. Because, an anything-goes type of culture does not recognize sin for what it is and will actually approve and promote it in the name of tolerance and acceptance (Romans 1). We do well to remember what Jonathan Edwards said: "You (we) contribute nothing to your (our) salvation except the sin that made it necessary."

DOES LOVE ALWAYS WIN?

Today a friend posted on Facebook a picture of a festive wedding cake with a pair of same-sex partners on top of the cake. She wrote: "I am an ally. No, I am not gay, bi, or trans. I just believe in the crazy notion that every single person should be able to live and love how they please without judgment against them. #CrazyNotCrazy #LoveAlwaysWins."

Does the world love better than the church? That is my question. Sadly, it has often seemed to be my experience—yet we supposedly have the love of Christ? How do we go about changing this?

I find myself divided, pulled on both sides by the legalism in the church and the license of the "CrazyNotCrazy" culture, and I find I really do not fit on either side.

I stand with Jesus to call all of us to love like He did, particularly as He did with the woman at the well. I have been that outcast woman, and Jesus has met me there at His well. I have received His love and acceptance and eternal gifts! I want Jesus, not religion, for everyone. Our hope is in Christ and His works of grace advancing in us to live what He does through us and being privileged to be His vessels.

SAVE OUR SHIP

A young man was raised in a devoted Spirit-led Christian home and had a close loving relationship with Jesus since he was a youngster. He was serious about his faith, his love for the Lord, and his lifestyle, so he stayed a virgin throughout his high school years. When he went away to a Christian college, his new roommate revealed that he was gay, happy with his lifestyle, and had no desire to live differently. Even though the young man did not state his disagreement unkindly, the roommate accused him of being unyielding and judgmental. Misunderstanding won the day.

A young woman raised in a Christian home eventually developed a lukewarm relationship with Jesus. She now questions why homosexuality and bi-sexuality are considered wrong. How can loving someone else ever be wrong? She has many gay and bi acquaintances and friends who seem like great people. Other people she knows have expressed gender confusion. The more she is around these friends, the more convinced she is that none of these behaviors are wrong and that Christians are unloving and judgmental—maybe even bigots. She has been around plenty of legalistic so-called Christians that have been gay bashers. Her acquaintances and friends are more loving than these Christians. She might even consider the same-sex scene herself.

Those stories might sound familiar to you.

Younger generation Christians want "love to win," and they celebrate the Supreme Court decision which changed the legal definition of marriage. This generation wants the church—people who say they are Christians—to love all people, including homosexuals and transgenders. In the view of these young believers, Christians need to be called out about their intolerance, judgmental attitudes, and their unlove.

They're not entirely wrong. Wasn't it Christ who said, "Love, as I have loved you?" (John 15:12).

It is difficult for those who haven't known anyone with gender confusion to understand the complexities of the issue. But no matter what generation we belong to and no matter what we've been taught before, each of us must learn to love in truth. And many of us need to repent of unloving and unkind thoughts and words. Jesus loved the sinners and was never reticent or fearful about interacting with them. Yes, He corrected error and self-righteousness and honestly spoke about sin, but he was always full of love and grace.

We are to love homosexuals and embrace them... but not exalt them. If homosexuality is part of your story, you need to be able to share about it. But that doesn't mean living it boldly: it means searching for the true Gospel and what it will do for you. It took many years for me to confess that same-sex experimentation is part of my story. Now as I tell you the truth of my past I hope to point you toward the guiding and cleansing, changing power of Christ.

The LGBTQ community is saying to the church, "If you love us, embrace us! Love not only us, but accept our belief systems."

Our message to this community needs to be this: "We love *you*. God loves *you*, just as you are. We embrace you, we know that Jesus died for each and every one of us. We're sinners too, and no better than you. We repent that we have acted as though we are. But we stand by our truth system, and can't embrace yours, though we respect you as individuals. We believe all transformation is possible through the blood and power of Jesus. We all still fall prey to our temptations and forget our shackles have been loosed; and to our shame, we choose sin. Some of us are gluttons, idolaters, adulterers, addicts to porn, and victims of eating disorders, etc. We don't always live victoriously. But if all of us will extend grace and mercy to one another, we can walk together through the temptations, lies, and shame, and can encounter the hope Christ came to give!"

ACCEPT NO SUBSTITUTES

True Christ-followers cannot live proudly and blatantly in sin. We must not approve sin or allow leaders to be in outright sin, extending a perverted grace mentality.

We are not to compromise the truth. We are to extend truth in love and grace and be willing to die so others can live. What the church needs to change is its emphasis on achieving salvation by our works. We need Pharisaism removed and the truth, based on the blood of Christ and work of Christ, as the main message.

Loving well is essential. Better the wounds of a friend (Proverbs 27:6). When you love someone, you speak the truth in love. We must not be complicit with sin. Genuine love confronts with the hope of restoring. Ignoring or denying sin is to put the person and community at risk. Care enough to say the hard things—and when done with love that truly desires what's best for the other person, this actually can build relationship.

May we show others, by our lives, the message that Jesus loves them and we do too. Jesus died to save them from judgment and wrath and to bring them peace. And He asks us to love like He loves and to forgive and serve as He did. Living out the example of love and forgiveness and truth to the world brings the Gospel of peace to the world. Christ is our peace in the midst of the war.

CULTURE WARS

Today's culture, often even inside the church, seems much like the book of Judges: everybody does what seems right in their own eyes. (See Judges 17:6; 21:25.) I've felt the hopeless despair of sexual sins and the post-traumatic shame hidden in a false works-based bondage inside the church. I was miserable. My experiences give me a unique vantage point and perspective—from my gender confusion, abortion, and experiences as a nurse—on the hopelessness of people caught up in sin. I have also experienced the lack of grace, acceptance, and love from the conventional church. I felt like a leper, unacceptable. Sadly, I have treated others the same.

Too often leaders address the truth, but they do so in such an upsetting, caustic, unloving way that it never brings peace, help, hope, love, or answers. I have been guilty of this, too. How do we fight the good fight of faith and stand against lies and sin in a loving way? How do we bring hope and healing in the midst of these cultural wars? By living the Gospel out in love and being willing to die for the lost while they are still in their sin. By being willing to get involved and do as the Holy Spirit directs you to do even when it is uncomfortable and costs you. For me, this book is a start.

On all fronts, true disciples are under siege. We are called not to bow to sin or make a peace pact with the enemy's ways or believe lies that will bring destruction. We are called to stand for truth, to know God's Word, to hold fast to the sanctity of life and covenant marriage, to love our enemies, and to pray for those that persecute us. (See Matthew 5:44.) Jesus is our model and tells us to follow Him.

OUR FOUNDATIONS

As followers of Christ, we need to rebuild the foundations of Gospel truth and herald the truth to all who will hear. We need

- zeal
- confidence in our own forgiveness based on the work of Christ
- determination to share
- lifestyles that are living proof that believing God is the best way to live, and
- an overarching passion and love for the Lord above all else.

These are the foundations that we must have to live as Christ taught us to live. We in the church are called to open the Kingdom of heaven to others. Christ is the key, the answer. Christ Jesus is Messiah King, and when we live Christ, we become the light of the world as Christ designed.

LIGHT OVERCOMES

As I worked on this chapter edit, it happened to be the weekend of the massacre in Orlando. A gunman with an assault rifle and pistol killed 49 people and injured 53 inside a gay nightclub. The incident is a travesty, an incredible tragedy. The spotlight was on crime against gays. Outrage was the response.

There were elements of hope. Susan Forbes, spokesperson for the OneBlood bloodbank, said 5,500 units were collected across the state to help the wounded. Chick-Fil-A responded by opening up on Sunday to serve Orlando. Just 3 months following the terror attack, Lead Them Home Ministries hosted nearly 200 evangelical leaders in the Orlando area at Posture Shift, a seminar designed to train pastors and ministry leaders to be more relational and more effective engaging the LGBTQ community. The brilliance of His light is seen.

We overcome evil with good (Romans 12:21).

EMBRACING LIFE TO BRING HOPE

Living as His light is the most fulfilling life possible. We want to share this with those who do not have it. The secret is first knowing and following Christ. Then understanding, embracing, and living Christ by the fullness of His Gospel. If we cut off those who are living in sin and do not receive them as Christ would, we are living like the scribes and Pharisees of Jesus' day. He said, "But woe to you, scribes and Pharisees, hypocrites! For you shut the kingdom of heaven in people's faces. For you neither enter yourselves nor allow those who would enter to go in" (Matthew 23:13, ESV).

 PRAYER

LORD Jesus, you are the Light of the World, and you call us to be the light of the world. We are your children of the day, children of light. Even though our culture may be on the brink of great disaster, you have set us as carriers of your light, so that whoever follows you will not walk in darkness. The all-surpassing power of the Holy Spirit, this treasure from God, indwelling those of us in Christ—convict our hearts of our own hypocrisy so that we may humbly bear witness to the culture around us of the truth of the Gospel and the hope you give to all who believe. May the message "You are loved" be displayed so deeply through us to all the hopeless—the abused, the addicted, the atheist—that they hear and see Christ in us to receive Him. May your love at the cross always win. In your name we pray, amen.

PART 3:
Elephants on Parade

"Look, Mommy!" the child exclaimed. "The elephants!"

The chaos of the circus and its lights and colors and crazy costumes seemed to stand still as the majestic train of tall, stately gray giants stepped forth, one foot after another, in rhythm with the music. They swayed almost gracefully as they lumbered around the rings. Each one carried the flag of a different nation and bore its colors on its back.

You couldn't help but stop and stare.

And with them walked their trainer, his eyes riveted upon them. Every step they took, his smile grew. A smile of pride. He knew how they had been, and it was their relationship and their time together that had changed it all. Now his work marched forward for the world to see—as much a display of the skill of their trainer as they were of the majesty and greatness of enormous pachyderms.

The circus had come to town.

The Kingdom has come to town. And we, parading heralds of the hope that our Father has placed within us, are more a display of His grace and love than we are a presentation of any goodness we think we might possess of our own merit. We are testimony to the nations of his power and love perfected in us, and our story, our testimony, is to draw the nations to Him.

For this, He has loosed our shackles. For this, He has saved us from the stampede. For this, He continues to beckon us onward in the relationship He has called us into: so we may herald His Gospel to the circus of this #crazynotcrazy world where #lovedoesntalwayswin.

GOD'S HOPE FOR HOPELESS STORIES

For God so loved the world, that he gave his only begotten Son, that whosoever believeth in him should not perish, but have everlasting life. For God sent not his Son into the world to condemn the world; but that the world through him might be saved (John 3:16-17, KJV).

"The Gospel of Jesus Christ is meant to be the best thing that ever happened to people and to nations. To stifle the Gospel does not just oppose God: it opposes all mankind." —Beth Moore, Children of the Day[28]

Those who sow tears shall reap joy. Yes, they go out weeping, carrying seed for sowing, and return singing, carrying their sheaves. (Psalm 126:5–6, TLB)

Revival is a renewed conviction of sin and repentance, followed by an intense desire to live in obedience to God. It is giving up one's will to God in deep humility. --Charles Finney

Being told you are forgiven and truly experiencing forgiveness are very different things. It took hitting rock bottom for me to come to a place where I could finally receive. I lived with suicidal thoughts, but I was committed to stay alive because deep within I knew it was God's will that I should live to testify. Satan's goal was to destroy me. I often repeated Psalm 118:17: "I will not die, but live, and I will proclaim what the Lord has done"(NET).

I did not walk the journey alone. God provided support for me as I continued to seek healing and battle depression. For several years I spent time with three precious friends every Thursday morning, seeking God in listening prayers and in the Scripture. They helped provide confirmation and support to seek professional help outside of our area. As a result of God's guidance, for fifteen years, I flew back and forth to Texas. Initially, I spent time in voluntary outpatient counseling, first at Meier Clinic and then at Samaritan's Well in Richardson, Texas.

But the stinging stigma of needing to receive psychiatric care and counseling caused further condemnation and another raw, painful, costly layer of shame. What kind of wife and mother was I? I was gone on a regular basis seeking help. My husband did not have his wife; my sons did not have their mother. My parents questioned my decision. My whole "support system" seemed to view me differently, or at least it felt that way to me. My sons especially were suffering along with me through my instability, through people's perceptions of me, through comments made by others, even church people. Someone even told them, "Your mother is crazy." I often came back with raw emotions, lacking full resolution, devastated anew as I pursued the necessary course of healing from the sexual abuse.

People didn't know how damaging their opinions, queries, criticisms, and statements were. They often served to reinforce the enemy's relentless mental torment in me. I wondered if perhaps I *was* insane, and I know that at the peak of working through the memories I did have of sexual abuse (memories of scenes that were right before and seemed right after), I fought for sanity sometimes daily.

I felt like a failure. A colossal mess of emotional turmoil.

Even though the comprehensive testing at Meier Clinic provided vindication that I was not crazy, I was struggling with depression and was emotionally volatile. I would ask for forgiveness and repent to my sons and my husband when I fell short, but that somehow hurt them, too. They saw my struggles, and my pain often transferred to them. I especially hate that I hurt my sons, but hurting people hurt people. The worst part was that it looked like my faith did not work. They saw me devoted to God's Word but defeated in my life. My faith and my repentance did not seem to translate into any sort of real victory, and that is the greatest heartbreak to me still to this day!

But there were and are bright spots: people who shine like lighthouses and have provided anchors in the storms through their prayers, support, and encouragement—in actions and in words.

I remember the very first day of counseling, I discovered how I was locked in shame—a prison of condemnation, misery, anger, and depression. So many of my issues stemmed from the trauma of my childhood. I struggled daily, listening to worship music and praying relentlessly. The sense of God's presence, His Word and power held me fast while some of His people were helpful supports, burning lights that drew me home to Christ when the waves were reckless and relentless.

And, after you have suffered for a little while, the God of all grace who called you to his eternal glory in Christ will himself restore, confirm, strengthen, and establish you. (1 Peter 5:10, NET).

Bella

During one visit in Texas, my husband came for a marriage counseling session. That weekend we joined my sister and her daughters to go see the new movie *Bella*. I had heard it was good, but not what it was about—a man, Jose, and a woman, Nina, who fall in love. Jose's history includes the accidental death of a child and Nina is experiencing an unplanned pregnancy. Nina feels alone, broken, and that she has no choice except abortion; but Jose uses the wounds of his past to help her through her pregnancy. As we watched I felt nothing, and I thought, *I must be healed!* I didn't realize I had emotionally disconnected.

The little girl in the movie Bella, looked so much like I had as a child it was unnerving. Even my sister leaned over to me and said, "It's amazing how much that girl looks like you when you were little. I can't get over it… especially since the topic…" Her voice trailed off. I stared straight ahead unmoving.

We weren't over it yet: we were damaged. We needed this message. God was taking me to the places of pain to heal me, not to nail my emotional coffin shut. As my shock faded, the pain took hold, and for a time afterward I couldn't function.

When my husband and I entered my counselor's office the next morning, I was in desperate need of God's help and grace. We were thankful for true Gospel ministered to us.

In time, we have come to realize we can be like Jose. We can open up our wounds, team up, and stand in the gap to show support to the Ninas of the world who think abortion is their only option. We can hold up the truths that can encourage them and potentially save them and their child untold hurt. We can show others that opening up and sharing our stories and testimonies can bring healing to them and to others. It offers bright, saving grace-hope.

Deadline

Another time, the Lord used the novel *Deadline* by Randy Alcorn to bring healing. One of the main characters, a reporter, attends a post-abortive support group for men as part of his murder investigation.

As I read the section of the book discussing the feelings of men who had insisted that the abortions take place, I realized with great sadness that I had not thought much about how my husband was feeling. It was a difficult yet very helpful process as it gave insights and brought things out in the open that had been hidden away for too long.

Before the healing came a severe time of trial: I saw my husband as an enemy, the perpetrator, and I saw myself as the victim. Worse was that to anyone else, it appeared my husband was a hero for staying with me—I knew I looked like the problem. I felt under judgment and a microscope from others and condemned without a real trial or others really knowing the truth.

I even begged the Lord to release me from the marriage—to give me a divorce. Over a series of distressing events and much prayer and searching, the answer I sensed from the Lord was this: "Yes, you can do as you want, *but* you will miss my full purpose for your life."

Wow—that stopped me in my tracks. I did not want to miss God's call. So I changed my "want to" to wanting to stay married, wanting God's will to be my will. Change was challenging. I had to stop thinking of my husband's sins as worse than mine and stop "making him pay" for what Christ had already paid for us both! It was a milestone of revelation. Our main need was forgiveness, and Christ paid for it fully. We both felt undone; bankrupt and inconsolable. A perfect storm for the real Gospel, but we had not learned how to fully apply the real Gospel to our lives yet!

It took dying to my flesh, my pride, my reputation (what little I had left) and living in Christ's forgiveness and grace by His Spirit. I asked my counselor to help me discuss the important parts of *Deadline*, with my husband, and asked them both to read the pertinent sections. My husband and I met with my counselor in prayer and deep discussion for two tough days. But the honesty was healing. My husband heard my heart and I heard his. We expressed our sorrow and repented earnestly, and deep forgiveness began. We connected in a way we hadn't since our very first year of marriage, decades before, when we destroyed our love and our baby! Why had it taken us so long?

God used the book to open his eyes, soften his heart, and end the denial that had kept us from truly moving forward. In the long run, it helped us come out behind our walls, denials, blame and begin to talk about the important things of the heart and know there was a way up and out. But "the long run" was very long and arduous.

My teen sexual sins and our abortion are the leprosies of our lives. Yet through the process of forgiveness and clearing our consciences through Christ, we have found the treasure of the Gospel. We can live righteously in Christ, experiencing His grace. We have not had further catastrophes, blights, or train wrecks of such enormity. Despite us, and only because of Christ, our shame is gone, our sins are forgiven, and our lives are transformed by the power of God for salvation because we believe in Christ as our Savior (Romans 1:16-17). For God so loved me, us, the world, that He sent Jesus so that whosoever would believe would not perish but have everlasting life and not be condemned! (John 3:16-17 paraphrased/partial.) I must never forget this truth. Satan works to try to diminish this fact from being felt and lived. God is love, and He extends this in all that He does! What an incredible invitation and gift of generosity God offers to us ALL! Living for God is the best life.

New Hope—New Setbacks

Even after all this, I still sometimes believed lies about myself and my husband. When memories were triggered, lies took hold because they still seemed true—shackles. I could not seem to consistently live in truth, forgiveness, and victory, no matter how much I prayed, read the Bible, or attempted to apply counseling. Releasing unforgiveness and choosing to believe the truth more than believing what my feelings told me was a constant battle. A turning point for me was when my counselor and a close friend explained that if I chose to hold onto unforgiveness, it was as if I were saying that what Christ did on the cross was not enough. If I chose to forgive, it would express the greatness of the work of Christ on our behalf. A reframing of truths: I could forgive for the sake of Christ's valuable sacrifice, to credit it to our account and to make what Christ did count.

I had felt that if I forgave, it was saying what we had done was okay, or that it was okay our baby was dead. I couldn't seem to get past this. But I learned I have to accept that our baby is in heaven, and that that was a choice we made! I cannot change those facts. What we did will never be all right. But to receive forgiveness and extend it to myself and my husband is to say Jesus' death paid the debt for the death of our child! It is to say the judgment we deserve was placed on Christ. That is good news, for we bear the judgment we deserve no longer. The Gospel in my life replaced the lies that we could not be forgiven and that we could not fully forgive each other. This enabled me to release our child into God's hands more fully and reframe the facts into the truth of the Gospel effectively. God's forgiveness at the cost of His only Son is the path to freedom. So I began to earnestly and purposely live forgiveness. It took Scripture, the will to choose love and forgiveness, as well as an act of God to accomplish what I could not do.

But a second setback to our healing happened in fall of 2014: my mom caught a cold that ended in pneumonia and heart failure. The same day she took to her bed, I got a call that I had been diagnosed with Arnold Chiari Malformation and may need to have brain surgery.

Within 14 days, Mom went home to heaven. I was heartbroken and grief-stricken, and the bodily sufferings I was enduring took a great toll. In the blur of loss and suffering, I battled depression.

My husband's loyalty, commitment, and love for me really began to warm and revive my struggling heart toward him. He cared for me and served me with compassion and love, especially when I was incapacitated with severe headaches, insomnia, and other related discomforts. He did all he could to alleviate the stress and help me to cope. I began to trust his love again.

And then... I began writing this section of this book. Revisiting these memories caused more trauma. I remember one specific day when I was irritable and edgy, and my husband asked what was bothering me. Answering his question required us to work through some questions and revisit some of the pain again, and it was hard. We talked about my doubts and fears, and how this book and telling our story openly to the world might affect us and my newfound growing trust and respect for him. I didn't want our relationship hurt or to have other people's respect or trust for him affected (one of the reasons I have chosen to use my given, birth first and middle name and my "in faith, imputed position based on Christ's righteousness" as my last name instead of my married last name, for now).

And the questions began. *Why is it so hard to write the truth? How will we deal with the world knowing our story? Will we go backwards in our relationship, and can our marriage survive it? How will this affect our sons and families? Am I really following God's leading?*

We've since been reassured of God's leading and protection. Still though, every step we take in faith.

Renewed Relationship

In the course of my healing, I began to rely on my husband to a different level than ever before. As I relied on him, I naturally began to receive his love and care in increasing levels. This renewed relationship was like gold mined from the cave of my physical suffering. Through his consistent help and presence, we began bonding and sharing. I told him the thoughts of my heart, my real feelings once again. I began trusting him to know me and love me unconditionally again. It was a vulnerable time, and sometimes it felt like it could kill me. To give my heart again and be known and loved again had seemed impossible, but God made it possible.

Overall we began to be restored to a place from before our disaster. While we may never have the relationship we had before, we do have something special now: real love and forgiveness, commitment, authentic intimacy, and the willingness to continue to grow and do the hard work of covenant relationships. We are content together.

Most importantly, Jesus is our Head, Center, and First Love. He is always with us and between us, bonding and uniting us and bringing forth forgiveness when we most need it. Having Jesus as our Savior, along with the prayer and Bible studies we do together, has kept us together. No question, we would not have made it or stayed together if we were not Christ followers. I may not be alive but for Christ.

Little by little we have been restored and redeemed. Recently we stood together for the first time to give joint testimony at a church. When I read him what I planned to share before the meeting, I saw again the pain it had caused him. I feel particularly sensitive and protective toward him, and I want people to know that he, too, was affected by my past. I remember telling him about the person who abused me when I was nine, and how I saw his sadness, pain, and anger. He has been devastated with me, grieved with me, and held me, believing in me even when others didn't. He has supported me in every way and in paying every bill. We continue to grow in understanding and forgiveness.

Our redeeming God has been so good to us. I have begun telling His story as it relates to my and our story. It is Good News. The greatest news that ever happened to me, to us, to the world, and I want everyone to know Jesus and His love and forgiveness.

God's work of redemption takes us out of our old life. It is a call to die to the old life and live a new life by His Spirit in us. In this new life, we are set apart and enabled to live in Christ's resurrection power by His Spirit. The world needs to be able to see God's plan of redemption manifested in our lives. Our born-again life is to be attractive and winsome to the world. We advance God's Kingdom by abiding in Christ and living with His full armor, daily fighting effectively against the schemes of the devil and resisting the evil day (Ephesians 6).

I knew that telling my story would be risky and costly. We need to count the cost because there is a cost. There are many rewards as well. I challenge you to look into the rewards that God promises.

FROM HOPELESSNESS TO HOPE

Transformations are the work of God. We are called new creations at salvation (2 Corinthians 5:17). At least this is what I see in my own life, as well as in the comparisons we continue to draw with the lives of Peter, Paul, and the Samaritan woman.

I notice the differences in the details of each of their transformations. Yet in each story, the true Gospel was at work "converting" them and their lives. Each one became a proclaimer of the Gospel with God's power and anointing. The greatness of forgiven sins, cleansed souls, and clear consciences prompted them to herald the Gospel. From their great sinfulness, the wonder-working power of the Gospel brought forth transformation and harvest! God promises this if we live out the true Gospel in His power! In our powerlessness, His power comes - when we live the true Gospel, we live the secret of hope!

I believe when we, like Peter, Paul, and the Samaritan woman, experience the greatness of Christ, His love and forgiveness, we will want to share this "best thing that ever happened" with everyone. We do not live in shame or guilt anymore—we want to share Christ. He is our treasure. Writing this book has brought me to treasure Christ more and more, and to live like these three and those like them. I too want Christ for all people.

Honesty

The Gospel doesn't "feel" true sometimes, even when I am on parade.

I am learning to talk to God more and more about how I feel. I don't deny the feelings. I am honest with how bad I feel and what I am thinking. But I purpose not to let my feeling rule me—even though they do, at times.

I read and meditate on God's truths in Scripture and I pray about my feelings. I pour out my heart to God. He knows what I feel better than I do. As I submit my feelings to God and resist the devil, the devil flees (James 4:7). Satan relentlessly tries to convince me of lies. I ask God to help me sort it all. I guard against allowing deception and feelings of unforgiveness or hate to enter and rule. I remind myself of God's unconditional love.

His love motivates my love for Him and others. "We love because He first loved us" (1 John 4:19).

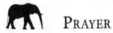 ## Prayer

God of all comfort, we praise your name above all names. Thank you, LORD, for who you are and what you have done for us. In the middle of our pain and affliction, help us feel your reassurance—and help us to comfort those who are in affliction with the comfort you have granted us. Help us live lives that are truly forgiven. In light of what we have done, what has been done to us, and the roads we have traveled, help us freely give the love, grace, and forgiveness we have received to others, at whatever cost to ourselves. Heal us of our brokenness, fill us with compassion toward those who need it, and help us, your Redeemed, to walk shoulder-to-shoulder with others on the road from hopelessness to hope. Help us live power-filled lives! Cause us to be worthy of your calling, and by your power, fulfill every desire for goodness and the work of faith (2 Thessalonians 1:11). In Jesus' name, amen.

Covenant of Hope

And God said, "This is the sign of the covenant that I make between me and you and every living creature that is with you, for all future generations: I have set my bow in the cloud, and it shall be a sign of the covenant between me and the earth. When I bring clouds over the earth and the bow is seen in the clouds, ...I will remember my covenant that is between me and you and every living creature of all flesh." (Genesis 9:11-17, ESV)

"The secret of the Lord is with them that fear Him and He will shew them <u>His covenant</u>" (Psalm 25:14, KJV).

"Hope," Beethoven cried, "you forge the heart into steel." Hope is confidence. Hope is determination. Hope is courage. And faith is the ultimate expression of hope. Belief fortifies the heart. The only source of true joy and peace is God Himself. The only way by which God can give any man joy and peace is by giving him Himself. A. Maclaren, D. D.

Now the God of hope fill you with all joy and peace in believing, that you may abound in hope, through the power of the Holy Ghost. (Romans 15:13)

Covenant is God giving man Himself.

In January of 2010, I attended the Passion Conference in Atlanta, Georgia. One morning before the conference began, I read about Cain and Abel. I experienced deep despair because I felt unforgiven. I had been like Cain, I had been coming mainly with my works, not through the blood sacrifice, really. Plus at the time, my life story held secret ugly parts that few knew about. I felt hopeless and guilty and overwhelmed with regret. I kept reading the book of Genesis and eventually came to the story of Noah. God made a covenant with Noah, promising that He would never destroy the whole earth with a flood again. The covenant was dependent on God's faithfulness. As I journaled that morning, I asked the Lord if He would make a covenant with me, too. Immediately after this I went back to the hotel room. The group leader, a friend, had left a book opened to a page for me to read.

When the glory of God touches the ugliest part of your life and uses it, there is no pride. Only awe.[29]

EVERYTHING FOR HIS GLORY

Reading those words was a milestone moment. My foulest skeletons that I've kept hidden and my most enormous elephants with their shackles are actually powerful tools in the hands of God. He will use everything for His glory. The next sentence in the book was a Scripture verse, "The secret of the Lord is with them that fear Him and He will shew them His covenant" (Psalm 25:14, KJV).

I was stunned. Minutes before, I had written my request to the Lord to make a covenant with me and now He orchestrated events to show me that He will show me His covenant. I experienced incredible hope in the unconditional love of God. I wanted His covenant to become real in my heart and life.

The key verse of the Passion Conference was Isaiah 26:8, "Yes, Lord, walking in the way of your laws, we wait for you; your name and renown are the desire of our hearts" (NIV). I repented that God's glory was not my desire. In fact, I was not even sure what God's glory was! I asked the Lord to make His glory my desire. Since then, I have prayed through this verse often. I made a trivet of Isaiah 26:8 as a reminder and marker of this event. It sits on my kitchen counter where I readily see it.

From that time on, the Lord surely has shown me His covenant. One book, Bible study, and message after another, He has been teaching me! I experienced God in a real way. The sacrifice of Christ fulfills the covenant and offers an experience of incredible hope in the unconditional love of God. I want His covenant to always be more than theology; I need it to be real in my heart and life. The reality of Christ is so much more than religion.

God's covenant sign to Noah was the rainbow. Noah and his seven family members were saved through the ark (Genesis 6). But the new covenant is a better covenant (Hebrews 8).

Today God's "ark" or rescue for man is the cross of Christ. "Whosoever" will believe in the work of Christ can be saved. At the cross, where Christ took what we deserve, Christ offers new life, a new covenant of hope. God's promise of a new covenant through the resurrection assures us of His faithfulness.

TRANSFORMING KNOWLEDGE

The essence of the entire Bible is covenant. Man's sin at the Fall broke the original covenant with God. Even though it was only man's choice, (God gave man free will but did not desire man to choose this way), that caused the chasm of betrayal and debt between Creator and Created, God, as the perfect, loving Father, paid all costs to restore His creation to Himself. I think of the New Covenant as what God does for man to be redeemed and restored. God gives His all, all of Himself. He empties Himself for us to be redeemed and restored (Philippians 2).

God intends to transform His creation into what He always meant it (and His children) to be. Further, He offers us rebellious sinners the opportunity to be a part of that transformation and to be members of His family. The issue: our need to be redeemed from sin and its penalty.

Jesus did what mankind could not do. Where man broke covenant, Christ Jesus fulfilled the covenant for man as fully God and fully man. The covenant God made with Abraham to bless the nations has been fulfilled in Christ.

The blood covenant of God is foundational, epic, and eternal: it allows us to know and understand our great salvation. This covenant gives us the greatest hope in the world; sadly, many in the church today often choose to live life rejecting that greatest of gifts. Life without covenant is life that requires fulfillment of the Law: an impossible task.

THE LAW KILLS

As I studied the concept of covenant, it became apparent that I had been living mostly by the Law instead of by the Spirit. The law kills, but the Spirit gives life (2 Corinthians 3:4-6). I had rarely depended solely on Christ for redemption and abundant life. I lived as I thought I was taught to live in the church—working for my salvation. The lifestyle failed me. I was living a foolish life of self-glory. I wanted New Covenant change in my living. I want to live true Biblical hope for the world!

SECRET COVENANT OF HOPE

In the King James, Psalm 25:14 reads, "The secret of the LORD is with them that fear him; and he will shew them his covenant." Notice that it begins with the phrase "the secret of the LORD"—this is important to consider and understand. First of all, we see that God has a secret. It's a safe place, a secret place He calls all of us to. In the secret of the Lord, we can openly confess our sin and find His favor; it's a place of the promise of hope of freedom, healing, and covering. This surely is related to the secret of hope we've been discussing.

Secondly, the all-capitals "LORD" is the covenant name for God. The Biblegateway.com dictionary puts it this way: "The word [covenant] is used with reference to God's revelation of Himself in the way of promise or favour to men."[30] God identifies Himself with covenant!

Covenant is so much who He is, He has tied it to the core of who *we* are as His beloved. God sees who He created you to be. Who you are in His Covenant is who you are in Christ. He is fully committed to you and bringing forth the completion of His vision for you.

And in the New Covenant, the requirements are all on Him. It's unconditional. God fulfills it. In a relationship of covenant, the relationship is more important than the needs of the individuals involved. He gave up His needs to provide for your needs, even when you do not meet the expectation of His standards. He committed Himself to you beforehand while you were still in your sin.

This is how we see the secret of hope at work in the story we've been exploring of the Elephant Gospel. The multi-layered secret of hope finds its basis in resurrection. Because in the shackled elephant's despairing place of brokenness, hopelessness, and emptiness—the valley of the shadow of death—that is the place we see Covenant at work.

John 12:24 says, "Verily, verily, I say unto you, Except a corn of wheat fall into the ground and die, it abideth alone: but if it die, it bringeth forth much fruit" (KJV). Where the grain of wheat dies, in fields of apparent barrenness, is where the secret of hope can spring forth! It is where the truth of "my powerlessness for His power" leads us past the stampeding elephants to the Kingdom advancement of the ever-growing elephant parade.

Our forgiveness is based on a Covenant understanding of Christ as our King, our Co-Heir, and our Bridegroom. This is the secret or mystery of Christ that the New Testament refers to over and over again. The New Covenant of God—my powerlessness for His power—is the secret of hope.

Just As I Am

From age 14-21 I secretly lived a life of sin and rebellion with no desire to change. I refused His grace and I rejected the idea of repentance. And I rejected the Savior in this sinfulness, even though I said I knew Him and knew He died for me.

His covenant love has always been a reality despite my unfaithfulness. Christ has brought me to a place of understanding His grace and mercy and His sacrifice at the cross that has changed me and brought breakthrough. Instead of wanting our judgment, He died to give us mercy while we were refusing repentance. Amazing grace! Living hope!

Today I am learning to be true to who I really am, *just as I am* in a small group of committed believers where we all are in authentic fellowship, true *koinonia*. Being with believers who love me is a gift and encouragement in my life. I am learning to live a 1 John 1 life; one of joy and New Covenant.

It has taken several years to develop deep authentic friendships with a group of likeminded believers. It was and is a difficult and painful process of vulnerability, rejection and at times great grief and pain. We are all just learning to live as 1 John teaches. It is not for the faint hearted. It is costly but worth it. Covenant costs. To love my friends for them, and not for me, costs me. As I love others the way Christ loves me, though, I experience Christ.

Satan is the father of lies. His big target is to try to deceive us about who God is, what God did, and what God says is true so as to destroy our faith. We must know God's Word, His new covenant, and know the love, grace and mercy of the cross. We must be able to defend our faith, speak up and stand firm as those of the truth, to prevail.

Living by the New Covenant is essential to living the reality of His incomparable gift of true love. Covenant brings breakthrough. Instead of being under judgment, we herald God's mercy, the messages that God is good which He proved at Calvary. To live out of gratitude for what Christ has done instead of living to earn salvation or fulfill obligation changes everything! Jesus died to save us—even while we refused to repent or fully leave a life of compromise, of sin, of wanting our sin more than our Savior.

He loves us above any love on earth and only holds back what will be harmful. The Father is a good, good Father and a generous giver by His nature. We need to live and give the messages of covenant hope.

God is Love

In 2006, sitting with my earthly father at the end of his life, I remember asking God if He loved me. Dad had fallen asleep and I was sitting there holding his Bible in my hand. I let it fall open, and the pages parted at Malachi 1.

> *"Here is the Lord's message to Israel, given through the prophet Malachi: "I have loved you very deeply," says the Lord. But you retort, "Really? When was this?" And the Lord replies, "I showed my love for you by loving your father, Jacob."*

My breath caught in wonder and awe. I felt God's love in that moment! I want this for others - others like me and my niece. There are so many of us who doubt or have in the past doubted God's love and questioned how to get free of the torment of feelings of purposelessness or worthlessness.

I remind myself of these truths: Christ overcame the world. He destroyed the work of the enemy. He did all that was needed for us to be reunited with the Father. He showed us the Father. Sin needed to be removed and Christ paid the penalty for our sin and redeems all who believe.

There is no greater love than one laying His life down for us. The two greatest commandments paraphrased: Love the Lord our God with all our heart, soul, mind and strength; and love our neighbor as ourselves. This is what we, as believers are to live. To love our neighbor, we need to love ourselves. For the first time I see so clearly how relentless God is in His covenant.

Too often, the world does not show love to people like us, the outcast or the addicted. They only see the addiction or burden, and they often don't see the person anymore. We are often looked down on, condemned, accused, belittled, treated with contempt or worse. This produces a loss of hope and a feeling of a loss of the Gospel. We need a hope renewal, a Gospel explosion. I pray for an understanding of the covenant of God to bless the world through His people.

I had not understood the enormity of my sin and the cost of it and was not living the gift of the forgiveness of my sins. I was ungrateful in my heart. I now see this. I now see this is also what had blocked my love for God! I was not living based on His covenant. God's response to Jacob pointed to covenant love. We need to live covenant love. It is the heartbeat of the secret of hope.

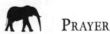 PRAYER

LORD, we thank you for making an unconditional, everlasting blood covenant (Hebrews 13:20) available to the whole world through Jesus Christ, the Savior of the world. Help us, your covenant-sealed people, go and share the greatness of Christ and the New Covenant relationship, the true Gospel as Jesus and Paul taught taught it and lived it. May we clearly make known and remember the broken body of Jesus Christ and His spilled blood for the atoning of our sins, the redemption of mankind. Thank you that we believe in Jesus, that He rescued us and offers us a better covenant based on His work, and not mankind's or other sacrifices. In this we can have unwavering hope. May the secret of your New Covenant be lived out by your grateful people who revere you, LORD, through their love, worship, living, and heralding the Gospel. Father, prepare us to be your sanctuary of hope, messengers of your New Covenant Hope to the nations. May many obtain salvation through our LORD Jesus Christ. In Jesus' name, amen.

HERALDS OF HOPE

To me, [though I am] the very least of all the saints (God's people), this grace [which is undeserved] was graciously given, to proclaim to the Gentiles the good news of the incomprehensible riches of Christ [that spiritual wealth which no one can fully understand] (Ephesians 3:8, AMP).

God is the only one who can make the valley of trouble a door of hope.
~Catherine Marshall

That which we have seen and heard we proclaim also to you, so that you too may have fellowship with us; and indeed our fellowship is with the Father and with his Son Jesus Christ. And we are writing these things so that our joy may be complete (1 John 1:1-4, ESV).

If you are going to walk with Jesus Christ, you are going to be opposed. In our days, to be a true Christian is really to become a scandal. ~George Whitfield

I will also speak of your testimonies before kings and shall
not be put to shame (Psalm 119:46, ESV).

After we experience redemption, God calls us to live and extend the true Gospel to ourselves and each other. This is the Great Commission (Matthew 28:19-20). I have discovered that only through understanding the New Covenant could I herald the Gospel effectively. May we all be a parade of unshackled saints, showing the nations the path to His throne!

THE FULL SCOPE

When we consider Christ's command to take the Gospel to the uttermost parts of the earth, we realize that there is much more at stake than we previously knew. The Gospel is established by and rests on our Creator's life, death, and resurrection and is infinitely valuable to individuals and to entire nations. Fully understanding the Gospel's eternal value affects our passion for Christ and the passion for souls to know Him.

The hope of the future depends on Jesus. The hope that the world will hear the Good News of Jesus depends on us! (Matthew 28:16-20)

HERALDING OR HINDERING?

Weighty thoughts and questions bombarded me as I thought on these truths. The power of the Gospel is available to be used each and every day. The cost of not taking advantage of that availability may be souls that are separated eternally from God. I especially questioned, "Am I hindering the Gospel, opposing God?" Sadly, I realized I have not heralded the fullness of the great salvation I have been given. I have hindered it and opposed the fullness of God's greatest gift. Heralding means to proclaim, announce, or publicize. I needed to wake up and fully declare the works of the Lord and live what I believe: the Gospel is the greatest gift and of first importance. The time is short.

DOOR OF HOPE

I have devoted time to studying ways to more effectively herald the treasure of Christ and His work to the lost world that needs him.

We have received extravagant grace, and our failure to herald it is scandalous. Each Christian makes a choice whether or not to truly walk with Jesus and share His Gospel of grace—knowing they will be opposed by the world, some in the church, and some in the dark kingdom of Satan. To receive Christ's salvation but not be willing to share His Gospel message is selfish. Sharing the Gospel message is the most loving, valuable, and blessed gift we can give to others—it's living proof that we understand the greatness of our own salvation. We are called to follow Christ's example. Our responsibility is to give the complete Gospel message of sin, repentance, and salvation. His sacrifice leads the way to the door of hope.

In His Word, God does warn us about the costs and the warfare that come with sharing the Gospel message. The more we share God's Gospel the more our lives will be attacked by the enemy because we are bringing God's Kingdom to enemy territory. Paul's life was attacked repeatedly. He was left for dead more than once. He was considered a fraud by the religious people of the day. Many wanted to destroy him. Jesus Himself was also attacked by the Pharisees who were filled with hate though He had done no wrong (Matthew 12).

HANDLING CRITICISM AND ACCUSATION

We learn a lot about handling criticism and accusation by observing Jesus' interactions with the Pharisees.

As we endeavor to let the Holy Spirit govern our lives, we will face some, even in the church, who behave much as the Pharisees did. We will be attacked. Those who are interested in defaming and harming us will not respond to our reasoning. We may need to confront them with the truth from the word itself, but ultimately we must recognize that hatred is a heart issue that arguments alone can't change.[31] Our job is to be prepared with the truth of salvation and the love of Christ. When we are secure in Christ we can face any attack. God will defend us. Our part is to be faithful as He leads and proclaim His name and message with truth, love, and grace.

TWO WOMEN

Mary Magdalene and the woman at the well were outcasts of society, but each one was accepted by Jesus, who saved and transformed each of their lives. As I think of these two women, I realize I am in good company. Maybe you are too. Jesus loves us no matter what our history. There is hope. In fact, hope surges from a closer relationship with our heavenly Father. These women were part of changing the world. Mary Magdalene walked closely with Christ and testified to His power and salvation. The woman at the well told her entire town about the Messiah she met at the well. They each received God's grace and heralded the Gospel to their world.

CHALLENGES

We cannot herald the Gospel without first living it ourselves, and we cannot live it if we are not in a personal relationship with Jesus—relying on the power of Christ alone to cleanse us and transform us. If we are timid about the blood of Christ, we will never be the overcomers John wrote about in Revelation 12:11. I have known Christ personally for many years, but I have not, until recent times, understood the importance of proclaiming my relying solely on the work of Christ on the Cross, the power of the blood of Christ for salvation. Thus I was hindering the Gospel in my own life and hindering it in those around me.

I have given testimony of my sins that Christ died to forgive, so others can know they too can be forgiven. I was snatched from the pit, and I want to make myself available to the Lord as He works to save others from their pits and shackles. I was saved by His death. I am saved by His Life and will be saved by His Sovereignty.

PAUL'S TESTIMONY

Throughout the New Testament, we read Paul's testimony. He told his story and lived the Gospel to groups large and small as a way to glorify Christ and advance the Kingdom. Scripture instructs us to give testimony—to herald the Gospel. Paul declared the enormous Gospel change in people who knew Christ.

"Or do you not know that the unrighteous will not inherit the kingdom of God? Do not be deceived: neither the sexually immoral, nor idolaters, nor adulterers, nor men who practice homosexuality, nor thieves, nor the greedy, nor drunkards, nor revilers, nor swindlers will inherit the kingdom of God. And such were some of you. But you were washed, you were sanctified, you were justified in the name of the Lord Jesus Christ and by the Spirit of our God (1 Corinthians 6:9-11, ESV)

When Paul met Jesus, he immediately began living his new life as a believer following Christ. He spoke and wrote his clear testimony in Jerusalem and beyond. We are to follow his example by giving testimony where *we* live and beyond. If God handpicked a religious zealot, murderer, and persecutor of believers, God is also willing to save anyone and work through them—including me. None of us are worthy—we just need to be willing. We must go out with this good news and herald the secret of hope to the world.

GREAT ARMY

True believers of Jesus Christ must unite to more effectively impact the world, not allowing the lies of the world to impact the church. Jesus wants us to love people as He loves them and connect them to His generous, merciful heart. He wants to assure them of His full forgiveness so that all guilt and shame is extinguished and His transformations happen. Heralding the Gospel in truth and grace is God's idea and command, for He wants none to perish.

RESURRECTION LIFE

The Christian life is a life of resurrection. My old life of hopelessness and sin was full of mistakes and pain. When I received Jesus' gift of grace and salvation, I died to that life. Jesus then began the process of sanctification. My new resurrected life is even better than a clean slate, because not only are my sins removed, but I also now have a *perfect* slate (Christ's slate of righteousness). God has forgiven and wiped away my sin, my past, my mistakes, my rebellion, my pain. In its place I have the righteousness of Christ and therefore I have hope. Resurrection is the pinnacle of the secret of hope. To live is Christ.

A resurrected life is an awakened life. (We must make sure it is not a resurrected lie or back to bondage we will return.) It is new life which leaves behind my old way of life. A life believing God's Word more than what I feel or what I can see or understand. My new life of hope trusts the resurrection of Christ, the power of God. To live this resurrected life in God's grace is to have a great awakening, to live true New Covenant.

THE GREAT AWAKENING

A friend's term paper about the Great Awakening began with this thesis statement, "Certain people of the Great Awakening inspired the seed of American independence." When I read that statement, it occurred to me that when God works through people by His Spirit, and as His people depend on Him, freedom results. In American history, freedom came as our founders declared their independence from the dead religion of England. Today, we find freedom if we separate ourselves from the dead religion found in some churches. This separation is what I believe God has been doing in me. Removing "me" and pushing the "Galatians-gospel mentality" out of the way, frees me from bondage and shame and brings me to an awakening of God's Spirit. The verse that comes to mind is "Not by might, not by power but by God's Spirit," Zechariah 4:6)

What surprises and scares me, though, is how quickly I can forget the freedom that Christ provides. I can so quickly forget the power and majesty of the Gospel, and the awe that it should produce in me. I confess that, I once had the thought, *I am tired of hearing that Jesus died and rose. It is the same message over and over.* I had begun thinking, *I am pretty good now; I don't need Jesus as much.* It is hard to admit that I allowed these thoughts to enter my mind. The Bible often tells us to remember and reflect on what God has done for us. Jesus helped me renounce those thoughts and the bondage they would produce. By the Holy Spirit, I put those thoughts to death and reminded my heart of the truth of God's Word and the work of

Christ. Satan wants us to rely on self and not rely on Christ's work. Satan's strategy for man to be self-reliant has made the church powerless. Dependence on self and not God's Spirit is a power-stealing strategy.

We read often in Scripture of idolaters. Though we hesitate to identify ourselves with worshippers of false gods, since golden calves are pretty uncommon these days, we aren't much different. We don't set up altars to gods who parade as such; rather, we set up temples to our own selves. Our altars might be our own little worlds or our own idea of perfection or idolatry- ones that might include sports, sex, alcohol, fame, materialism, beauty, education, careers, or even ministries, whatever displaces our Lord!

If we herald the Gospel as we are called to do, our stories spark the awakening to life as we declare our independence from the shackles and idolatries that have held us back.

NOT ASHAMED

You and I must be vigilant to stay awake, slaying any thought that would try to diminish Christ or the cross. I have spent hours thinking about what Jesus suffered, the agony Christ endured for the forgiveness of my sin. Our focus must be on Christ and Christ's love and atonement. We have been given much grace. The more we focus on Christ and His Work for us, the more we will love Christ, herald the Gospel, and live in His truth and victory.

> For I am not ashamed of this Good News about Christ. It is
> the power of God at work, saving everyone who believes (Romans 1:16, NLT).

Jesus is our Savior. He is the Messiah, the Anointed One. He alone can bring us eternal life and reveal truth. Nobody can go to the Father except through Jesus the Son. Our message is His truths and our job is to exalt Christ and His cross and show the way to Christ through repentance at His cross and redemption completed through his resurrection. Paul's greatest boast was Christ crucified. Yet his attention on the resurrection was clear and unmistakable and essential to the Gospel: 1 Corinthians 15:12-20; Romans 4:25; Acts 17:30-32; Acts 23:6-9; Acts 24:14-16 and also 2 Timothy 2:16-18

According to my friend's term paper, "the true definition of spiritual awakening is the sovereign moving of the Spirit of God untouched by anything except God's grace and mercy. Spiritual awakenings change society through the work of the Holy Spirit and the unrelenting prayers of believers." George Whitfield and Jonathan Edwards were *not* the reason for the Great Awakening, but each of them had experienced a great personal great awakening. As each man followed Christ, God's Spirit and His grace and mercy worked through them mightily to bring the truth and herald the Gospel to the people. These men prayed an outpouring of prayers, and the Holy Spirit moved.

How I want the Spirit to move in me more fully, to the level of the Great Awakening revivalists! May God bring us all to live the New Covenant and experience a Great Awakening and revival! God alone can produce this, but we are to herald His message and live the New Covenant!

ALIENS AND STRANGERS

At salvation, we are made citizens of God's Holy people, members of God's holy family.

> Now therefore ye are no more strangers and foreigners, but fellow citizens with the saints, and of the household of God (Ephesians 2:19, KJV).

We will be hated by the world and not be of the world any longer, but chosen out of the world.

> *If the world hates you, you know that it has hated Me before it hated you. If you were of the world, the world would love its own; but because you are not of the world, but I chose you out of the world, because of this the world hates you (John 15:18-19, NASB).*

> *They are not of the world, even as I am not of the world (John 17:16, NASB).*

Paul had a very deep experience of the indwelling and the work of the Holy Spirit, when he accepted Jesus Christ as Lord and Savior. I desire this same revelation to be more evident in my life and in the lives of believers everywhere.

Finding righteousness in Christ alone and living by the Holy Spirit was a dramatically different experience. Paul was given revelation of God's grace in a way we may not fully understand until we enter heaven ourselves. Prior to his experience on the Damascus Road, Paul thought he was doing all the right things, that he was better than others—especially those of "The Way," the first Jewish Christians. He also held to the cultural Jewish prejudices of being set apart from or above the Gentiles. This elitist, privileged attitude caused a hostility between Jews and Gentiles.

Legalism influenced Paul's life and the same legalism is evident in the Pharisee-type Christians of today. I am sad to say I bought into this attitude for too long and became a deluded hinderer of truth. Legalism and the elitism it produces exert a malignant influence.

Paul understood, by revelation from Christ, that this attitude had to go. God changed Paul radically. He wrote:

> With Christ as my witness, I speak with utter truthfulness. My conscience and the Holy Spirit confirm it. My heart is filled with bitter sorrow and unending grief for my people, my Jewish brothers and sisters. I would be willing to be forever cursed—cut off from Christ!—if that would save them (Romans 9:1-3, NLT).

Because of the magnitude of what Christ had done for him, Paul had a passion for Christ, His Gospel, and the people He came to save. I am challenged by Paul's words. Am I ardent about my faith and audacious about loving Christ? Does my heart break for those that have not received Christ's forgiveness? Does my life show that I know hell is real and I don't want anyone to perish? Do Christ, His Gospel, and His love of people define me? The true Gospel was Paul's overarching passion, and he changed the world through the power of the Holy Spirit.

Turn the World Upside Down

After Pentecost, Paul and Peter turned the world upside down. They became vessels that the Holy Spirit filled with power from on high to bring about revival in the world. I believe if they were interviewed today, they would clearly point to the work of God, not to their own work. They would fully agree that God raised them up, filled them up, and awakened them to His reality, His covenant, and the riches of His inheritance.

Christ's love was and is the greatest love there is—especially considering who He is and who He loves—and He showed His love for me by dying in my place. He is pleased when I give testimony of His great grace, love, and forgiveness. It is a glorious day to live in the truths of this great salvation and we are to want this for all people. He carried my sins far away. It is a reason to rejoice. I love the song "Glorious Day" by the group Casting Crowns. The Gospel is in the refrain. He lived to love us, died to save us, was buried to bury our sins and rose to justify us. Staggering love, matchless covenant, eternal love. It is a clarion call—brilliant and clear—to His majesty and the magnitude of His love and grace.

GO AND TELL

There are people waiting for a rescue, both physically and spiritually. All believers are called to go and tell the Good News. Will you be one? For me, telling my story is the call God has placed on my life for this season. I firmly believe He has called all of us to tell our stories as a way to give Him glory and to help others to overcome. Heralding the Gospel and living the love of God encourages others to be honest with their stories. A great work of God can result. Life springs forth from death. Freedom springs forth from slavery. Hope in the hopeless rises through the power of the Gospel.

 ## PRAYER

Dear LORD, help us to herald the Gospel even when we face accusation, criticism, or opposition. Give us the heart like Jesus, Thank you for making us one with Him, united with the Father just as He prayed for us in John 17. Let us pass on to others the message you gave to us. So others can accepted it and know that Jesus came from you, Father, and will believe you sent Him. Give us the courage and voice of the woman at the well who told everyone she knew about you. Awaken us so that we will turn the world upside down for you. As we tell the Good News, open the door of hope for those who are lost, confused, troubled, miserable or needing rescued, saved from spiritual death. Birth faith in multitudes to be born again. Help us to be willing to tell others who you are and what you have done for us! Holy Spirit, lead us as we break our silences and tell our stories in the light of Christ's story. Change our lifestyle to faithfully live your covenant. In Jesus' name we pray, amen.

AUDACIOUS HOPE

Oh! men and brethren, what would this heart feel if I could but believe that there were some among you who would go home and pray for a revival - men whose faith is large enough, and their love fiery enough to lead them from this moment to exercise unceasing intercessions that God would appear among us and do wondrous things here, as in the times of former generations.
- C.H. Spurgeon

Therefore, since we have such a hope, we are very bold. (2 Corinthians 3:12, NIV)

"The Christian life, if it is grasped according to God's truth, is a magnificent obsession with an eternal hope, a hope that does not lead to an escapist attitude, but to the pursuit of life on a whole new dimension. It makes you bullish, as we might say today, on the potentials of this life as stewards of God. It gives us power to live courageously, to be all God has called us to be in Christ." Hope. Bible.org

New Birth to Joy and Holiness
3 Blessed be the God and Father of our Lord Jesus Christ! By his great mercy he gave us new birth into <u>*a living hope through the resurrection of Jesus Christ*</u> *from the dead, 4 that is, into an inheritance imperishable, undefiled, and unfading. It is reserved in heaven for you, 5 who by God's power are protected through faith for a salvation ready to be revealed in the last time. (1 Peter 1:3-5, NET)*

The law works fear and wrath; grace works hope and mercy. Martin Luther

Peace and Hope 5 Therefore, since we have been justified through faith, we have peace with God through our Lord Jesus Christ, 2 through whom we have gained access by faith into this grace in which we now stand. And we boast in the hope of the glory of God. 3

Not only so, but we also glory in our sufferings, because we know that suffering produces
perseverance; 4 perseverance, character; and character, hope. (Romans 5:1-4, NIV)

Wildly exuberant fans fill huge sports stadiums. Cheerleaders shout and dance, inspiring excitement and enthusiasm. Some people jump to their feet in great anticipation, filling the air with cheers at all decibel levels. Most are dressed in team colors to show their team spirit, some even with painted faces and bodies. So much energy expended in a frenzy of activity—all for the love of the team, its players, the game and the win.

Communities anticipate and cherish these arenas of competition. They live for the next game! The energy of the crowd and their shouts and whistles of approval spur the participants on, and the fans feel alive with a common purpose. The experience offers a soul-stirring environment, contagious hype, emotional highs, waves of unity, joy, and enthusiasm. In the stadium, we feel the freedom and encouragement to voice passion for a common mission, community, and shared love. Why? Because we love contests, camaraderie, and the display of real talent. Maybe the cause is worthy and important because it is our school, neighborhood, or city. Most commonly, though, there is a desire to invest in and be part of what we think is greatness.

And why not? The desire to be part of a team, and to give it all for a victory delights us and increases the enjoyment of the experience. Fans are single-minded in their support, motivating the team and spurring them on to win. The players do all they can to win. They "feel the fire," driven by the fans' passion and energy. The coaches work even harder to motivate the team to even greater accomplishments and success—all to win a game.

Pulse-Pumping Joy

Have you ever wondered what would happen if the body of Christ had this kind of passion, zeal, and unity—the drive and determination inherent in a thriving team community where people know Christ and the eternal souls that are at stake?

I have. I have obsessed over it. What if we really realized the greatness we have in Christ? What if we loved our Lord above all, enjoying His presence and power? What if we worked together, following our Creator and Savior, supporting His team to win? Whether fan, cheerleader, or player, our focus would be to bring glory and honor to the name of our Lord and Savior.

We have the Holy Spirit in us to work far more than what we are able to do ourselves. In Christ, we have fellowship with God the Father. We are one with God through Christ. It is our theology, but is it our reality? We have so much in Christ, so much more than any counterfeit the world offers. This in-Christ reality and its joy, power, and authority should give us passion and oneness that is far above any sports crowd's enthusiasm.

The Bible encourages us, "we ought to give the more earnest heed to the things which we have heard, ...*so great salvation*; which at the first began to be spoken by the Lord, and was confirmed unto us by them that heard him; God also bearing them witness, both with signs and wonders, and with divers miracles, and gifts of the Holy Ghost, according to his own will?" (Hebrews 2:1-4, partial paraphrase from the KJV, emphasis mine).

We are talking about God and His so-great salvation. Can a sporting event even begin to compare? Someday, will we stand before Jesus and wonder why we had more passion at a sporting event than in our worship of our eternal God, His eternal gift and Kingdom, and the salvation of our eternal souls?

Great joy comes from knowing Christ, being fully indwelt by His Spirit, and loving and worshiping the Lord. My mentor sent a quote from Joni Erickson Tada, "When we're gripped by the fact that God lives inside us, pulse-pumping joy splits the seams of our soul, and we can't help but act a little foolish."

AUDACITY

The word *audacious* has been used to describe Margaret Sanger's views.

> "[Our objective is] unlimited sexual gratification without the burden of unwanted children... [Women must have the right] to live ... to love... to be lazy ... to be an unmarried mother ... to create... to destroy... The marriage bed is the most degenerative influence in the social order... The most merciful thing that a family does to one of its infant members is to kill it[32]."

Her shocking statements have appealed to many and impacted generations: she became the founder of Planned Parenthood, an organization with much influence today.

It is time for Christians to be audacious—in a different way. Our audacious, radical love for Jesus fills us with His love for the people of the world in grace and truth. We are called to bring hope to all and to speak up for justice and for the way, truth, and life.

MIRACLE OF HOPE

"Think of ways to encourage one another to outbursts of love and good deeds" (Hebrews 10:24, NLT). Christ and His abiding Spirit motivate us and bring us together in a deeper, more significant way than the world offers. When we show how we are different—indwelt with God's Spirit, in Christ—others will long for who and what we have.

Jesus said, "I have prayed for you that your faith may not fail. And when you have turned again, strengthen your brothers" (Luke 22:32, NIV).

"When a death-overcoming Savior prays that your faith does not fail, know that He has the power to help you maintain your faith. No matter how low you may have fallen, you can stand in Jesus's keeping power. You can turn again because Jesus, who is risen from the dead and seated at the right hand of the Father, is praying for you. He wants you and embraces you, even when it feels like you have nothing to offer; when you feel like you've ruined your chances." [33]

LIVING WATER

At the well, Jesus revealed His identity as Messiah and said whosoever drinks of the water that he gives them shall never thirst (John 4:14)—the water that Christ gives is a well of water springing up into everlasting life. He also declared we are to worship in spirit and in truth.

As I survey the wondrous cross, the Prince of Heaven hanging there for me, I can't help but want to be audacious for Christ. There is no greater love than the love of God. (See John 15:13, Romans 5: 7-8, 10, Song of Songs 8:6; Matthew 5:44; Luke 6:35.)

HOPE AGAINST ALL HOPE

What happens when your hope runs dry, and any hope you can muster seems contrary to reality? Hoping against hope may seem ridiculous and foolish on all human accounts.

BUT GOD.

In God, all hope is available even when our human hope seems gone, absent, and completely dead. He is in the impossible. He has conquered sin, the curse of death, Satan, hell, and the grave. He raises the dead! So God brings hope when all human hope falls short and is extinguished.

It is still mustered "hope against hope." We must choose to place our hope in God, not in ourselves or our own abilities. Our powerlessness for His power: the secret of hope. When I am bankrupt, empty, unable, empty of self, at the end of my hope, then I come before God knowing that He can do what I cannot. And when He comes through for me, I will know beyond the shadow of a doubt that it was completely Him—not me at all!

In Romans 4:17-19 we read a New-Testament account of Abraham and Sarah and their hope-against-hope (also found in Genesis 15, 16, and 18).

Against all hope, Abraham in hope believed and so became the father of many nations,
just as it had been said to him, "So shall your offspring be." (Romans 4:18, NIV)

Abraham, the father of the Jews—though he was close to a hundred years old and his wife, Sarah, was ninety—chose to believe that God could do what He had promised and give them a child of their own, through their own bodies.

And God did. He sent Isaac, their miracle child. By faith we believe in the resurrection power of God! Where we as humans fail, Christ comes through—always has, and always will. Even when it doesn't look like it from a human perspective, from heaven's point of view, it's a sealed done deal.

False religion says, "Get 'er done!"

Christ says, "It is finished."

"We believe!" Hope cries out.

This is that New Covenant, the imputed righteousness we see in Romans 4. It's not earned; it is given. It is not the reward for performance; it is *received*, not achieved! This is hope realized through Christ. It is not law; it is grace. Our salvation is the great hope-giver. The rewards of salvation are riches more amazing and valuable than anything life on earth can offer. On top of all that, there is the added joy of being with and knowing Christ. He satisfies with living water and provides assurance of our future with Him. If you know Christ, you know hope. Hope anchors the soul (Hebrews 6:19).

 PRAYER

Father, fill us with audacious hope in Christ. Thank you for the gift of being the bride of Christ, as your believers. Help us to be prepared for the joy of the holy wedding day in our future and live today as your bride making herself ready. Help us live daily by first knowing we are saved by God's work and then by putting our faith to work. Increase our love for you and our believing in your word by faith, as Abraham did. Help us overcome temptations through your presence reigning *in* us as we allow the Holy Spirit to reign *over* our mortal body and mind and will. Help us trust your lordship, because we love you, and live a life of incredible, audacious hope. LORD, Help us live New Covenant Hope, In Jesus' name, amen.

CONCLUSION:
A FINAL THOUGHT ON HOPE

One final story.

Mary and Daniel have an abiding, close relationship with Christ. As born-again committed believers, they have lived their lives with love for Jesus, and it shows. They held fast to their desire to remain sexually pure, and they married as virgins. At their wedding, guests experienced God's presence, joy, and love. As they exchanged vows, the audience witnessed pure, sacred, lovely covenant faithfulness. They washed each other's feet at the altar, displaying their desire to show humility and service in their marriage. Their first dance brought people to tears for they radiated a sense of how God meant it to be. How blessed and beautiful; how tender and precious. The favor of God was evident.

The fight for purity and to overcome temptation is a struggle. Mary and Daniel upheld God's foundational truths of purity, honor, and integrity in covenant marriage and showed the blessedness, reward, and joy that God's way is the best way.

What a contrast with so many of the stories we have discussed in this book! Their story glorifies God because Mary and Daniel deliberately chose to accept and follow covenant truth.

But even if your story is one of brokenness—even if your past is scarred, and your elephant shackles still shame you—know that when you embrace covenant living, God sees you and your story under the defining blood of Jesus Christ. Your wounds can heal, and your scars can announce His coming and His transformational power!

We see this cycle with Jesus as well.

Christ's places of greatest despair and hopelessness brought us hope. When he cried out, "My God, My God, why have you forsaken me," He was enduring the wrath and rejection our sin deserved—so we could be extended grace and acceptance. His relationship with the Trinity was broken—and this was a burden we will never be able to comprehend.

Christ's death and resurrection allowed for the reversal of the fall of man and the reign of sin, which the first Adam ushered in. Christ was forsaken so we would not have to be. From His places of greatest hopelessness, He birthed our hope. Thus, our greatest places of defeat and sin can be exchanged for Christ's righteousness, forgiveness, acceptance, and His love. The story of our hopelessness and how Christ overcame can be the birthplace of hope for others. Ours is a great salvation.

In summary, I reiterate: I lived most of my life thinking that all I needed to do was be good. My past failures and sins left me feeling that I needed to be extra good all the time. It's been a long journey. I've tried to make others love me. I've tried to make God love me. I could never measure up to the standards that I put on myself. When I meet someone who is legalistic and judgmental, I see myself in their false, hypocritical, and superficial spiritual life. When I came to the end of myself and saw my sinful heart in the light of Jesus, I gave up trying and accepted grace. Giving up on our self-dependence enables God to enable and empower. When you give up on yourself and your own works, then faith to believe in the Lord Jesus and His works comes.

God is called "the God of Hope." This means He is the source of all real hope. If we are without Christ, we are without God and without hope (Ephesians 2:12; 1 Timothy 1:1-2). If we are going to have hope, which is confident expectation, it must come from Him, for He alone has the power to give it (Psalm 62:5). Without Christ, there is no hope (Charles Spurgeon).

That is the secret: we have to know we have broken covenant with God, but Christ was broken for us and fulfilled the covenant for us. He brings spiritual life and power to us by filling us with His Spirit. Our powerlessness for His power!

I pray that my places of failure help others discover God's faithfulness as they identify with my story, my sins, and my failures, and discover God's mercy and grace. I hope you see that Christ restores and redeems. The elephant, once-shackled, now proudly marches to herald the Good News to the nations.

Expect great things from God, attempt great things for God. –William Carey

*It is the duty of those who are entrusted with the Gospel to endeavor
to make it known among all nations. –William Carey*

May we "enlist under the banner of Jesus" as Spurgeon beckoned in his last sermon:

*Those who have no master are slaves to themselves. Depend upon it, you will either serve
Satan or Christ, either self or the Saviour. You will find sin, self, Satan, and the world to be
hard masters; but if you wear the livery of Christ, you will find him so meek and lowly of heart
that you will find rest unto your souls. He is the most magnanimous of captains. "There never
was his like among the choicest of princes. He is always to be found in the thickest part of the*

battle. When the wind blows cold he always takes the bleak side of the hill. The heaviest end of the cross lies ever on his shoulders. If he bids us carry a burden, he carries it also. If there is anything that is gracious, generous, kind, and tender, yea lavish and superabundant in love, you always find it in him. These 40 years and more have I served him, blessed be his name! and I have had nothing but love from him. I would be glad to continue yet another 40 years in the same dear service here below if so it pleased him. His service is life, peace, joy. Oh, that you would enter on it at once! God help you to enlist under the banner of Jesus even this day! Amen.[34]

Special Prayer for the Heralds of Hope
Based on Psalm 119:46; 1 Thessalonians 2:4; 2 Timothy 1:4, 8-14; and 2 Timothy 1:11; Hebrews 10:23, Revelation 22:17,20,21 (HCSB)

LORD, help us not be ashamed to testify about you or those that share in suffering for the Gospel. May we continue to preach, regardless of the circumstances, in accordance with your invincible power. Thank you for delivering us, saving us, and calling us with a holy calling—a calling that leads to a purposeful, set-apart, consecrated life, not because of our works or because of any personal merit, since we could do nothing to earn this, but because of Your own purpose and grace, which was granted to us in Christ Jesus before the world began.

But now that extraordinary purpose and grace has been disclosed *and* realized by us through the appearing of our Savior, Christ Jesus, who through His incarnation and earthly ministry abolished death, making it null and void, and brought life and immortality to light through the Gospel. We therefore are appointed to go and share this Good News regarding salvation. So help us, God, to reap a great harvest.

This is why we suffer as we do. Still, I am not ashamed; for I know Him and I have believed, with absolute confidence in Him and in the truth of His deity. Cause us to be persuaded beyond any doubt that you are able to guard that which I have entrusted to you until that day, when I stand before you.

LORD, help us keep and follow the pattern of sound teaching in the faith and love which are in Christ Jesus. Help us guard, with greatest care, and keep unchanged, the treasure, that precious truth, which has been entrusted to us (that is, the Good News about salvation through personal faith in Christ Jesus), through the help of the Holy Spirit who dwells in us. Bring us to speak of your testimonies before kings. We believe that we shall not be put to shame.

Holy Spirit, protect the good treasure you have entrusted to us, that we may love, live, and give the Gospel we were gifted to give. Empower us and indwell us. Help us honor Christ as holy, always ready to make a defense to anyone who asks a reason for our hope.

For we speak as messengers, approved by God to be entrusted with the Good News. Our purpose is to please God, not people. He alone examines the motives of our hearts.

For this Gospel I was appointed a herald and teacher. Cause us to herald the Gospel in

Your power and harvest as Paul and the first apostles did. Let us hold fast the confession of our hope without wavering, for He who promised is faithful. The Spirit and the bride say, "Come." Let all who hear, all who are thirsty, come and take the living water of hope freely. In Jesus' name, amen.

He which testifieth these things saith, Surely I come quickly. Amen. Even so, come, Lord Jesus. The grace of our Lord Jesus Christ be with you all. Amen.
(Revelation 22:20-21)

APPENDIX:

FOR THE THOSE WHO MADE THE DECISION TO ABORT

Grief and regret from abortion is the most common experience in our culture today.[35] Because it is such an integral part of my own story, I want to offer a final testimony to any readers who have themselves survived this atrocity.

My situation is somewhat unique and yet with some similarities to the majority too. I wanted our baby, but I caved to my husband's insistence for abortion our first year of marriage. For years following, I could forgive neither myself nor the father of our baby—my then and now husband who has loved me consistently for more than 35 years. I have his permission to share this story but have not used our last name to protect our children and him.

As a review of common known facts regarding post-abortion aftermath: Suicide rates, psychiatric problems and post traumatic stress syndrome is known statistically to be increased in post abortion women.[36] Most women that have experienced abortion end up not staying with the father.[37]

A majority of women interviewed post-abortively report being co-erced, forced or persuaded into the "choice" of abortion and it not truly being their choice.[38,39] Keeping an abortion or abortions a secret can prevent individuals or couples from receiving the help and love and support they need to heal and move forward. Domestic violence increase has been associated with abortion secrecy and lack of healing involved in dyfunctions associated.

"Unfortunately, all the evidence shows that abortion to "save a relationship" almost never works. Many relationships between couples come apart shortly after an abortion. Others survive only because the partners are still bound together by grief. These relationships often turn into prolonged, mutually destructive mourning rituals.(1) Even married couples are often driven apart by an abortion unless they can find a way to complete the grieving process together.

Abortion breeds anger, resentment, and bitterness toward the partner who was not supportive or who ignored their partner's desire to keep the baby."[40]

This last paragraph, basically describes our marriage and our story. I just so would have liked someone to have told us before the abortion and that we both had listened! Thankfully, by

God's grace He is completing the grieving process "together in us" and bringing redemption. "The Gospel re-enacted in marriage", Tim Keller, (quoted in "HOPE FOR THE FAMILY" THE GOSPEL, HOPE, AND THE WORLD [DR. TIMOTHY KELLER | Sermon transcript, 18 October 2009] I believe, is known to say. I wanted our baby, but I caved to my husband's insistence for abortion our first year of marriage. For years following, I could forgive neither myself nor the father of our baby—my then and now husband who has loved me consistently for more than 35 years. I have his permission to share this story but have not used our last name to protect our children and him.

I needed to gain the freedom that truth brings. The secret of hope, which I repeat often, is Christ's full forgiveness and exchanging our powerlessness for His power through living the Gospel fully. That message will be beneficial to those struggling to forgive themselves or others for decisions that have negatively impacted their life. Sixty-four percent of women who have had abortions were coerced or forced. So much for choice. Women who felt they had no choice because boyfriends, husbands, parents, and others made the decision.

And when these women repent, please change to: In my opinion and by my experience in hearing feedback from some of the women who have expressed repentance and sought healing at church, there is a risk of being doubly victimized by the contempt of religious people or pastors who do not extend true Gospel grace. Feelings of guilt and condemnation and even suicide can result.

But here is my message for you: we do not have to live with the shame or guilt anymore. That is why I can write these things—because He has taken them away. Forgiveness does not mean that there are no consequences, yet even in them, there is hope. God knows all and He cares. He has promised redemption, and Romans 8:28 is an assurance and comfort. There is hope in His many promises. Hope in the inheritance, which He promises. Knowing Christ is eternal life and abundant life.

Christ Forgives All

The first time I remember hearing a great biblical answer on abortion on the radio was program Open Line with Dr. Michael Rydelnik[41]. He spoke to a caller named Barbara. She shared her experience and then stated, "Here is the sin I committed that I just don't think is forgiven." (Deep inhale of surprise from Michael) Then Michael, the radio host, said to her:"Barbara, let me reassure you, if you have trusted Christ as your Savior, and it sounds like you have, and if you did that from reading Romans, it is hard to imagine a whole lot better book to read and get saved by….that's a wonderful thing, and let me propose, as serious a sin as I think abortion is, there is FORGIVENESS for that: the BLOOD OF CHRIST CLEANSES US FROM ALL UNRIGHTEOUSNESS for those of us who have trusted CHRIST. And so, you have been forgiven that as well. There might be consequences that you will continue to carry but they will not keep you out of heaven.

The broadcast concluded with a discussion on the book, Out of the Salt Shaker. It was said that the author, Becky Pippert wrote "we shouldn't be surprised when a murderer is forgiven because all of us have had a hand in killing our Savior!"....And so you know, but for the grace of God, who of us would be saved?

GIVING TESTIMONY

When we give testimonies of our abortions, we will have the opportunity to tell of the work of Christ on our behalf. I have much in common with pro-choice people because of my experiences. I was a victim of sexual abuse and I had an abortion. As a nurse, I took care of a baby who had survived a late term botched abortion while I was about 5-6 months pregnant myself. I believe that the Lord wants me to be a bridge to the pro-choice camp—to tell them about the common experiences but give them hope because of Christ.

Most pro-choice individuals don't want to talk to a pro-life person because, frankly, we have been judgmental and unloving. But the two camps agree on more than you think. Many agree on giving healthcare to born-alive infants who survive abortion. We could work together on that issue. It would be a start.

Building bridges should be easy for us because we know that we were no different from pro-choice individuals, until Christ changed our hearts and lives. With Christ we are to be filled with love and humility and forgiveness extended in grace and mercy.

As those who have walked this hard road, our stories give us even more potential to herald the Gospel for God's glory.

THE SECRET OF HOPE

I had been invited by one of the women in Bible study to attend a Republican luncheon with her and her husband and their foster baby. Her husband was adamantly opposed to abortion. It was my first time meeting him, but I told him a brief account of my story. He thanked me—with tears in his eyes—for trusting him and sharing my story. He said if more people were transparent like I had been, maybe we could end abortion. It was the first time someone encouraged me.

It has been said that there are three gifts a mother gives a child. Birth. Unconditional love. Knowledge of Jesus. As I thought about this in light of our need to accept those who have painful pasts, I believe there are three gifts we can give. 1) Knowledge of the sanctity of human life. We are eternal beings who have been created in the image of God. 2) The incomparable and unconditional love of God that is shown in Christ Jesus our Lord. 3) His desire for us to be with Him and the plan of salvation that He has implemented.

If we offer these three gifts, we will stop abortion from within. God is pro-life, and He hates the shedding of innocent blood. And even if some who are pro-choice bring death, He offers forgiveness, life and eternal hope through his New Covenant.

When we are in Christ, we are a new creation, the old is gone and the new has come. And if we confess our sins He is faithful and just to forgive our sins. Thank you Jesus for the hope we have in you.

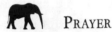 ## Prayer

LORD, we don't know where we would be without your love, your compassion, your forgiveness, and your hope. Thank you for making a way where there was no way. Heal us, LORD, and use us. Use us to bring an end to the death of innocent babies. Use us to encourage those who face difficult decisions. And especially, LORD, help those who have had abortions to recognize that you love and want to forgive them and that you died to make their forgiveness possible. Please help those men and women who experienced abortion (especially ones that did not want one), to forgive all involved in the decision. We thank you for the hope that only you can provide. In Jesus' name, amen.

SUGGESTED RESOURCES

ARTICLES

"The Bible and same sex relationships: A review article." Tim Keller, June 2015. http://www.redeemer. com/redeemer-report/article/the_bible_and_same_sex_relationships_a_review_article

"How to Be Born Again." Billy Graham. <https://billygraham.org/story/how-to-be-born-again/>

BIBLE STUDIES

Breaking Free. Beth Moore. Lifeway Christian Resources, 2009.

Children of the Day. Beth Moore. Lifeway Christian Resources, 2014.

Covenant: God's Enduring Promises. Kay Arthur. Lifeway Christian Resources, 2009.

Mercy Triumphs. Beth Moore. Lifeway Christian Resources, 2011.*One In a Million: Journey to Your Promised Land*. Priscilla Shirer. Lifeway Christian Resources, 2009.

What Love Is: The Letters of 1, 2, 3 John. Kelly Minter. Lifeway Christian Resources, 2014.

A Woman's Heart: God's Dwelling Place. Beth Moore. Lifeway Christian Resources, 2007.

Hope for Wholeness: Freedom from Homosexuality through Jesus Christ. <www.hopeforwholeness.org>

BOOKS

Battling the Prince of Darkness: Rescuing Captives from Satan's Kingdom. Evelyn Christenson. Victor, 1990.

Deadline. Randy Alcorn. Multnomah, 1994.

I Saw the Lord: A Wake-Up Call for Your Heart. Anne Graham Lotz. Zondervan, 2006.

I Said No! A Kid-to-Kid Guide to Keeping Private Parts Private. Kimberly King. Boulden, 2008.

Jesus > Religion (Why He Is So Much Better Than Trying Harder, Doing More, And Being Good Enough). Jefferson Bethke. Thomas Nelson, 2013.

The Secret of the Forgiveness of Sin and Being Born Again. Pastor Ock Soo Park. Good News Publishing, 1997. Available for free download at <http://www.goodnews.or.kr/en/2message/html/books/bornagain.pdf>.

The Secret of the Lord: The Simple Key That Will Revive Your Spiritual Power. Dannah Gresh. Thomas Nelson, Inc., 2005.

The Secret Thoughts of an Unlikely Convert. Rosaria Champagne Butterfield. Crown & Covenant, 2012.

Undaunted: Daring to Do What God Calls You to Do. Christine Caine. Equip and Empower Ministries. Zondervan, 2012.

Undaunted: One Man's Real Life Journey from Unspeakable Memories to Unbelievable Grace. Biography, Josh McDowell. Directed by Cristóbal Krusen. Tyndale House Publishers, 2011.

Understanding Sexual Identity: A Resource for Youth Ministry. Mark Yarhouse. Zondervan 2013

SERMONS

"The Blood of the Everlasting Covenant." Sermon. Spurgeon, C.H. http://www.spurgeon.org/sermons/0277.php

"Hope for the Family." Sermon. Timothy Keller. <http://www.gospelinlife.com/hope-for-the-family-6035#.WAOOQ4nFyQw.facebook>

Sermons by David Wilkerson, Carter Conlon, Patrick Pierre, William Carrol, Teresa Conlon, Ben Crandall. Times Square Church. <www.tscnyc.org>

"Taking Hold of the New Covenant." Sermon. David Wilkerson. Times Square Church Sermons. <www.tscnyc.org>

"Hope for the World." Timothy Keller. Gospel in Life, 2009. <www.gospelinlife.com/the-gospel-hope-and-the-world>

"The Centrality of the Gospel." Timothy Keller. Gospel in Life, 2016. Series: Where We are Going: The City and the Mission. www.gospelinlife.com/the-centrality-of-the-gospel-9225

VIDEO RESOURCES

Audacity. Film, directed by Ray Comfort. 2015. Available for free download. <www.audacitymovie.com>

Bella. Film, directed by Alejandro Gomez Monteverde. 2007.

"The Broken Way." Video, Ann Voskamp. October 2016. <https://www.facebook.com/AnnVoskamp/videos/1347910035221167/>

"The Broken Way: An Interview with Ann Voskamp." Jonathan Petersen, Biblegateway.com. October 28, 2016. <https://www.biblegateway.com/blog/2016/10/the-broken-way-an-interview-with-ann-voskamp/?utm_source=bg&utm_medium=email&utm_campaign=weeklybrief&spMailingID=52640717&spUserID=ODg2NjQwMTUwMDAS1&spJobID=1025376722&spReportId=MTAyNTM3NjcyMgS2>

"On the Farm with Ann Voskamp." Interview, Charles Morris. October 23, 2016. <https://www.youtube.com/watch?v=EPSkxBNNUOQ&sns=em>

Such Were Some of You. Documentary, directed by David Kyle. Pure Passion Media, 2014. <www.SuchWereSomeOfYou.org>

Websites

Authentic Intimacy. Intimacy resource by Linda Dillow and Juli Slattery. <www.authenticintimacy.com>

Lead Them Home Ministries. <http://leadthemhome.org/> Email: info@leadthemhome.org

Mastering Life (Pure Passion TV). <www.MasteringLife.org>

New Hearts Outreach, Tampa Bay. <www.nhotampa.org. >

Parents and Friends of Ex-Gays & Gays. <www.PFOX.org>

Ravi Zacharias Ministries. "A Slice of Infinity." <http://rzim.org/a-slice-of-infinity/>

Walls Down Ministry. <https://www.wallsdown.org/>

REFERENCES

1   Moore, Beth, *Sacred Secrets*, (Nashville: Lifeway, 2013), p. 10.

2   Moore, Beth, *Sacred Secrets*. DVD. (Nashville: Lifeway, 2013).

3   Bethke, Jefferson. *Jesus > Religion*, (Nashville: Thomas Nelson, 2013), p. 78-79.

4   Altrogge, David M. *3801 Lancaster: American Tragedy*. Documentary. 2015.

5   "Sexual Abuse: A Major Cause of Homosexuality?" *H.O.M.E.* http://www.home60515.com/3.html

6   "Sex Trafficking," *Polaris*. Accessed November 25, 2016. https://polarisproject.org/sex-trafficking

7   ibid.

8   Graham, Billy, "Value of Your Soul," *Decision* Magazine. July 28, 2012.

9   Moody, Dwight. *Sovereign Grace: Its Source, Its Nature, and Its Effects*. Original publishing 1891. Public Domain.

10 Ensor, John, and John Piper. Interview with Lecrae Moore. January 3, 2015. http://www.desiringgod.org/interviews/passion-life-interview-with-lecrae

11 Graham, Billy. "Answers." June 24, 2010. Accessed November 25, 2016. https://billygraham.org/answer/i-wish-i-could-believe-god-will-forgive-me-but-i-cant/

12 Moore, Beth. *Breaking Free*, (Nashville: Lifeway, 2009), p. 214

13 Dillow, Linda, Slattery, Juli, *Surprised by the Healer*, (Chicago: Moody, 2016), p. 7.

14 Butterfield, Rosaria. *The Secret Thoughts of an Unlikely Convert*, (Pittsburgh: Crown & Covenant, 2012), p. x.

15 Lucado, Max. *Confession*, podcast audio. December 3, 2012. Grace. https://maxlucado.com/listen/confession/.

16 Frangipane, Francis. *The Shelter of the Most High*, (Lake Mary, FL: Charisma House, 2008).

17 *Living the Story*. General editor Dan Woldmoth, (Wheaton: Crossway Books, 2007).

18 Henry, Matthew. *Matthew Henry's Commentary*, "Phil 3:18-19." https://www.biblegateway.com/resources/matthew-henry/Phil.3.17-Phil.3.21

19 Deffinbaugh, Bob. "Peter's Sermon at Pentecost (Acts 2:14-36)," Bible.org. Published November 17, 2005, https://bible.org/seriespage/4-peters-sermon-pentecost-acts-214-36.

20 Strauss, Lehman. "The Pentecostal Experience - A Study in Acts 2." Bible.org. Published May 25, 2004, https://bible.org/article/pentecostal-experience-study-acts-2

21 Wiersbe, Warren. *The Bible Exposition Commentary*, (Victor), p. 525-526.

22 Lotz, Anne Graham. *I Saw the Lord*, (Grand Rapids: Zondervan, 2007), p. 50.

23 Ibid., page 46-48

24 Warren Wiersbe. *BE Series, Volume II*, p 436.

25 As quoted in –Timothy Keller, *The Prodigal God* (New York: Dutton, 2008), 46.

26 *www.stjohnssav.org/wp-content/uploads/2014/11/Lesson-9-The-Singer.pdf*. Accessed 11/25/16.

27 "The Story." *The USS Indianapolis*. Accessed 11/25/16. www.ussindianapolis.org/story.htm.

28   Moore, Beth. *Children of the Day: 1 & 2 Thessalonians,* (Nashville: Lifeway, 2014), p. 55.

29   Gresh, Dannah. *The Secret of the Lord: The Simple Key That Will Revive Your Spiritual Power.* (Nashville: Thomas Nelson, Inc., 2005).

30   "Covenant." Dictionary, Biblegateway.com, accessed 11/25/16. https://www.biblegateway.com/resources/dictionaries/dict_meaning.php?source=1&wid=T0000916.

31   "Jesus, the Cornerstone." *Today in the Word.* March 26, 2016. Accessed May 18, 2016. http://www.todayintheword.org/titw_devotion.aspx?id=181482.

32   Sanger, Margaret (editor). *The Woman Rebel.* Volume I, Number 1. Reprinted in Woman and the New Race. New York: Brentanos Publishers, 1922.

33   Parnell, Jonathan, *When Jesus Prays for Your Faith,* February 12, 2015, http://www.desiringgod.org/articles/when-jesus-prays-for-your-faith.

34   Spurgeon, C.H. Sermon. "The Statute of David for the Sharing of the Spoil." https://www.ccel.org/ccel/spurgeon/sermons37.xxvii.html

35   Ensor, John, and John Piper. Interview with Lecrae Moore. January 3, 2015. http://www.desiringgod.org/interviews/passion-life-interview-with-lecrae

36   Charisma Magazine titled Abortions Can Cement a Relationship, Suggests 'Cosmopolitan' Mag 11:30AM EST 1/31/2014 JENNIFER LECLAIRE

37   After abortion.org Can Relationships Survive After Abortion? Dr. Theresa Karminski Burke

38   http://clinicquotes.com/statistics-on-coerced-abortions/

39   http://www.theunchoice.com/pdf/FactSheets/ForcedAbortionFactSheet.pdf

40   After abortion.org Can Relationships Survive After Abortion? Dr. Theresa Karminski Burke

41   "Open Line" with Dr. Michael Rydelnik, Saturday, June 14, 2014.